THE INDEPENDENT MASTER OF ARMS

THE INDEPENDENT MASTER OF ARMS

Le Maîstre d'Arme Libéral

CHARLES BESNARD

translated by Chris Slee

The Independent Master of Arms
Copyright ©2021 Chris Slee (translator)

ISBN: 978-0-6452538-1-8 (eBook)
ISBN: 978-0-6452538-0-1 (Print)

Le Maîstre d'Arme Libéral, Charles Besnard. The original text is from a facsimile of the 1653 edition. It is asserted this book is in the public domain.

Created at LongEdge Press, first edition.

To all members of LongEdge Fencing for
their continual inspiration.

Contents

Introduction

Besnard in Context

Charles Beanard was born in 1615 and died on 17 June 1675. Although his place of birth is not known with certainty, it is known that he flourished and eventualy died in Renne, Britany. He claims in his text to be a proud Breton and there is no reason to doubt this. HEMA practitioners and re-enactment groups in the region are in the process of scouring the local archives for more information about the man and his life.

His text was first published in 1653 and centres on the use of the court sword and foil and, in this manner, may be thought of as the beginnings of the smallsword tradition and the school of the *escrime française*. Certainly, the weapons pictured in the engravings refer more to the smallsword than to the long rapier of the previous generation.

Besnard's France was dominated by court politics in which various factions and individuals jockeyed for position and power. The Thirty Years War, which saw the Most Christian Kingdom of France enter the conflict on the side of the Protestants against Catholic Spain, had ended fifteen years ago but the fallout from the Treaty of Westphalia had yet to settle. The King, Louis XIV, came to the throne in 1638 at the age of four under the regency of his mother, Anne of Austria. Even though he achieved his majority two years before Besnard published his text, the king declined to rule in his own power until the death of his mentor, Cardinal Mazarin, in 1661. The Thirty Years War and two half-hearted civil wars, the *fronde parliamentaire* (1648-49) and the *fronde des princes* (1650-53), had almost bankrupted the country. Nevertheless, France went on, under Louis, to become the wealthiest, most powerful and most aggressive nation in Europe until the Revolution.

Besnard's Fencing

The sytle of swordsmanship described in Besnard's text diligently maintains a separation between offensive and defensive actions. This is at odds with swordsmanship following a more traditional Italian approach in which all defences must also provide an attack in the same tempo. With this change alone, we can see the move towards a style of fencing much more like the smallsword texts of a generation later.

Besnard presents a mix of the long lunge and the half-thrust (also called the thrust on the firm foot). The long lunge, presumably an Italian import, provides the means of striking the opponent wheras the half-thrust is used as a mid-way testing position to determine the opponent's reaction to the initiated fencing action. At times, Besnard calls out the half-thrust as the first tempo of a two part attack. At other times, the half-thrust is a notional midpoint in the development of the attack as a single fencing action.

Besnard is terribly fond of enumeration and creating lists. It is evident in the layout of the text, which is divided into four parts. The first chapter deals with the sword, the stance and basic actions, all outlined with the help of a carpenter's or mason's plumb-bob to ensure the student's limbs are making the correct angles. The long second chapter deals with the meat of his teachings with the sword, covering attacks and defences in certain types of engagement. The much shorter third and fourth chapters object to duelling with pistols and knives as the literal work of the Devil, created by the Fiend to rob France of its prowess and reputation.

It is in the second chapter that the man's love of list-making is highlighted. There are four engagements and, although he largely discounts but does not ignore engagements in *première* and *seconde*, he concentrates his teaching efforts on the usual engagements, those in *tierce* and *quarte*. In each of these two latter engagements, after subjecting the opponent's blade, the opponent has four options for reacting to this: do nothing, disengage in order to subject, disengage in order to attack, or remain in engagement and subject the attacker's wepon using force. Each of these reactions generates a subsequent list of actions the attack may take to capitalise on the opponent's movement and intention. For instance, there are nine set counters to the opponent's intention to disengage in order to attack.

The second chapter is itself divided into two parts. The first outlines the manner of seeking engagement in order to take advantage of the opponent's reaction as touched on above. The second shows the reverse and the correct manner in which to deal with an attacker who follows the strategy of engagements in the first part of the chapter.

In all, Besnard's text is a well thought out and presented outline of court fencing in the middle of the seventeenth century.

The Missing Pages

This volume contains a translation of four pages which are missing from commonly available scans and transcriptions. This situation only came to light when comparing online scans of Besnard from different sources. These pages give the definitions for a number of actions and specify the stance and manner of holding the weapon.

In one case, the missing pages changed the meaning of the text and work was required to visit all usages of the term and translate these passages again. The missing pages give the definition of the term *quarter* as a synonym of the fencing action also referred to as a *volte*, a species of the Italian *inquartata*. Earlier versions of this translation rendered *quarter* as a verb meaning 'to thrust in *quarte*'. While not entirely incorrect, this rendering certainly lacks the full sense of the term that Besnard intends.

Translation

Besnard's text is very easy to read. He writes in a fairly clear and definitely very straightforward, conversational style with little literary allusion or complex grammatical constructions. One aim of this translation is to capture this feeling.

In the French of the period, one does not simply strike or hit an opponent. One 'gives,' or 'throws,' or 'pushes' one's point onto or, more disturbingly, into the target location on the opponent's body. These words are used interchangeably in the text and so I have made no distinction between them and the more prosaic 'strike' in the translation. Similarly, one is never hit by an opponent's attack; it is 'received.' Occasionally, the original term has been used where it seems appropriate.

The guard positions and thrusts are named in French *première, seconde, tierce* and *quarte*; in English first, second, third and fourth. I have retained the French term when the word refers specifically to a technical fencing action and used the English term when the main sense is ordinal.

One of the difficulties encountered with Besnard's use of these words as technical terms is that the reader must decide whether he is talking about, say, your opponent's thrust in *tierce*, i.e.: a thrust with the fingernails turned downwards, or your opponent's thrust to the opening on the reader's person in the *tierce* position or line. Both are expressed as 'your opponent's thrust in *tierce*'. Where this is not obvious from the context, it has been footnoted.

Translating an inflected language such as French into a generally periphrastic language like English presents some challenges in that the former has a richer vocabulary of inflected pronouns and conjugated verbs with which to make its meaning. This is obvious in the translation where certain subject and object pronouns have been replaced by the subject or object to which they refer in square brackets, [].

At all times where there is potentially a decision to be made about how to interpret particular word choices by the author, the original text has been footnoted. Some commentary may be included if necessary.

Acknowledgements

This book was not posible without the help of my dedicated and super-skilled editor, Lois Spangler. If my translation makes any sense at all it is due to her efforts.

The engravings in the original text were faithfully reproduced by Lenny and Keagan from Fox & Balloon Designs (https://foxandballoon.com/).

Selected References

Académie Française. 1695. *Dictionnaire.* Paris.

Broist, P., Drévillon, H., Serna, P. 2002. *Croiser le fer: violence et culture de l'épée dans la France moderne (XVIe-XVIIIe siècle).* Champs Vallon, Seyssel.

Cotgrave, R. 1611. *A Dictionarie of the French and English Tongues.* Adam Islip, London.

Joyce, M. 2015. 'A Short Study of the Smallsword', *The Combative Corner*, 16 February 2015 [blog]. Available at https://combativecorner. wordpress.com/2015/02/16/a-short-study-of-the-smallsword/ (accessed 17 August 2021).

THE INDEPENDENT MASTER OF ARMS

The Independent Master of Arms

Treating on the theory and exercise of the sword alone, or foil, and of all that which can be done and practised more subtly, including the main figures and postures in intaglio engraving.

Additionally containing other advice[1] on this subject.

Made and composed by Charles Besnard, a Breton living in the town of Rennes and teaching there the above-mentioned exercise.

Dedicated to Our Lords of State of the Province and Duchy of Brittany.

At Rennes

At Julien Herbert, Printer and Bookseller, rue Saint Germain at the image of Saint Julien.

1653

With the King's privilege.

---

[1] *moralités.* Cotgrave includes the sense of philosophical advice.

To Our Lords

Our Lords of States of the Province and Duchy of Brittany

My Lords,

One cannot but know that our illustrious Armorica has always been a rich nursery for and the noble nurse to the greatest men-at-arms who, on very important occasions, have appeared in this great Kingdom and in foreign wars. And as we are the children of these illustrious heroes, we have a strict obligation to be the heirs to their virtues and their courage, since we are to them their victories and the sweet fruits of their triumphs. That is why, through this little work, I have done my best to collect the chief maxims of skill and virtue that must be followed, and the vices and faults that must be avoided, in order to imitate them and make us worthy successors of our victorious Ancestors, to preserve in our century and to transfer to our posterity the titles of honour that they have successively acquired and preserved from century to century until us. And since I only undertook this little work through the zeal to preserve and to augment (to my ability) the glory of this province, of which I can call you the fathers and preservers, it will be, if it pleases you, my lords, all the more acceptable to you that it comes from one who is obliged to you to contribute to the honour of the nation through right of birth. I am promised that your illustrious names placed on the front of this little treatise will render it not only more acceptable but also will serve it as a defence against the envious, and as an assured safe conduct in order to have it pass usefully through the hands of individuals and into future centuries, which is one of my greatest desires for all who talk with me (with respect).

My lords,

Your humble, very obedient, and very faithful servant and subject of the province of Brittany,

CHARLES BESNARD

To the Reader

Friend reader,

Although ordinarily one passes over prefaces and the advice that one is accustomed to put at the beginning of works,[2] in order to start the discussion, I cannot refrain, however, from giving you this admonition that I believe is absolutely necessary both for your own satisfaction as for my particular interest, which obliges me to pray you to excuse the barbarity of some words which are neither common nor absolutely French that I have nonetheless used because they seem to me more expressive and suit better the matter that I am dealing with. Besides, I beg you to believe that without being clear[3] about the light and knowledge that my profession and my experience have given me, I cannot conduct the work to its perfection with such economy and schooling.[4] As a man who has lived all his life in study and closeted, you will oblige me extremely to not censure my work with such rigour and severity that you could do to a man who had been raised and nourished in the schools and from whom you would expect a more elaborate work. And be assured that I would be very greatly rewarded for my vigils if my labour can pass for mediocre in your judgement.

Farewell.

Extract from the King's privilege

By the grace and privilege of the King, given at Paris on the sixteenth of September in the Year of Grace one thousand six hundred

---

[2] *mettre à l'entrée des lieux*, Literally, "put at the entrance of places"
[3] *que n'étant éclairé que*
[4] *avec tant d'économie et d'école*

fifty-three and the eleventh of our reign. Signed for the King in his Council, Chassebras,[5] and sealed in yellow wax with the Great Seal. It is permitted to Charles Besnard, resident of the town of Rennes, to have printed a book entitled "The Independent Master of Arms etc" for the period of five years. And very express prohibitions and prescriptions are made to all printers, booksellers and others of whatever quality and condition that may be to print or have printed, sell or distribute the said book during the said time without the consent of the said suppliant or having his reasons on pain of three thousand *livres* fine and confiscation of copies. Because it is our pleasure, as previously charged, to put them on sale, to put two copies in our public library, and one in that of our very dear and loyal Sir Moley, Knight, Keeper of the Seals of France. These present letters may be held to be duly served, as is more fully declared in the said privilege.

Final printing on 25 October 1653.
Copies have been provided.

---

[5] Could refer to Gabriel Chassebras, Magistrate at the *Cour des Monnaies* between 1665 and 1675.

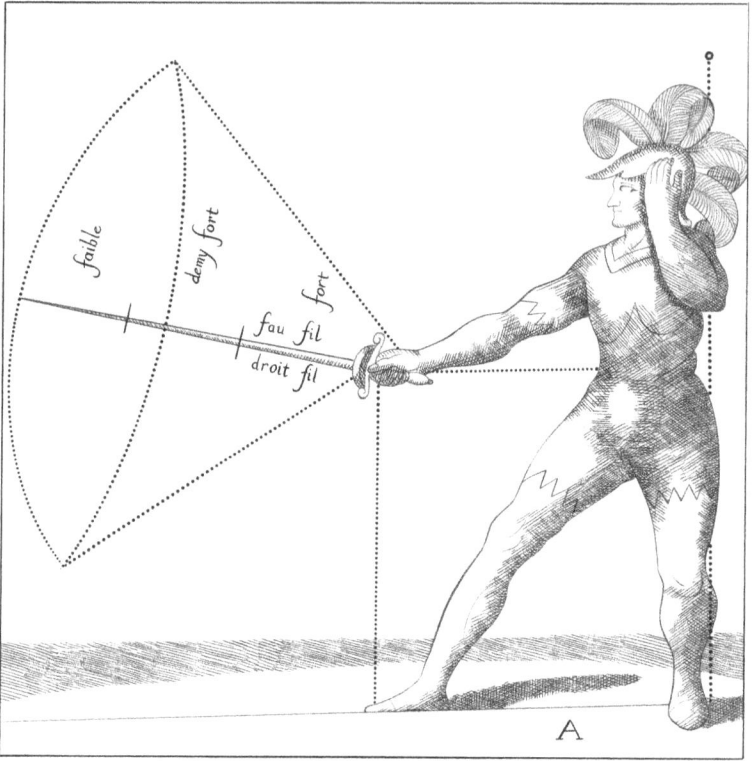

faible

demy fort

fort

fau fil

droit fil

A

The Independent Master of Arms

Chapter I

In which the principles of the art and the exercises of the sword alone or foil[6] are dealt with, and how one should put oneself into guard and a balanced posture.[7]

To put oneself properly in guard and posture in order to do the exercises of the sword alone or foil, it is necessary first to put the sword or foil such that the thumb is placed on the cross or flat of the sword and the index finger is under the flat of it in a semicircle and directly under the thumb and to firmly close the hilt with the three other fingers. And afterwards, put oneself in guard in this fashion.

It is necessary to present the whole body sideways[8] before your opponent. Put the left foot behind, crosswise,[9] bending the left knee and hip[10] in such shape that the point of the shoulder covers in a descending straight line the point of the knee, and the point of the knee [covers] the point of the foot. It is necessary to hold the left arm in a circle and the hand high with complete freedom, the back of which may be turned towards one's opponent, and placed at the height of and in line with the left ear or eye, and that the whole body is balanced and supported with the left foot without any constraint.

One should present the right side and also hold it straight without making any bends from the shoulder to the foot. The point of this foot is turned forward to face one's opponent, the heel lying on the line and

---

[6] *fleuret*
[7] *posture avec proportion*
[8] *tout le corps de côté*
[9] *de travers*
[10] *pliant le jarret et l'aine gauche*

9

facing the ankle of the left foot. The right arm (the hand of which will hold the sword in the manner already said) is also extended forward, but so that it may be a little bent in order to have greater freedom [of movement]. The wrist with the sword guard is held and placed straight above the point of the foot and not to the side, neither outside nor inside.

Finally, in order to be properly in guard and in a balanced posture, it is necessary that the Mathematical rules must be met in it. Namely, that the two points of the feet make a right angle with the heels. There are again two shapes and figures of angles which are made, one by the bend of the knee[11] between the heel and the point of the buttocks,[12] and the other by the bend of the hips and the points of the shoulder and left knee.[13]

These [following] three perpendicular lines must also be kept and observed, which one can do with the lead at the end of a string which architects use, putting the line against the back of the point of the shoulder, letting the lead drop. It is necessary that the ankle of the foot, and the outside of the thigh of the leg equally touch the said line.

Similarly, when putting the same line in front of the point of the shoulder, dropping it to the point of the left foot, it is necessary that the point of the foot, of the knee, of the shoulder also equally touch the said line.

And although the left side may be thus bent and contracted, it is nonetheless necessary that the right side (as has been said) be held straight, and without making any bend, and that this line gives again this proportion, namely, that having the foot advanced, the arm extended in front, and the wrist held above it, putting again the plumb line against the guard of the sword at the thumb, so that lead which is at the end of it touches the point of the right foot.

It is necessary to say again here at what height the wrist must be placed, because from the movement of the wrist depends the execution of the skill of the sword. For, if he should make disengagements, beats and parries, it is with this [the wrist] and for all that, (he) should neither remove nor swing the arm in any manner.

Finally, the wrist must do through its movement that which the centre of a turning wheel does, which through its movement without changing its position, finding in an instant the extremities of the circumference high, low, to the right and to the left.

The wrist does the same, making the point of the sword work

[11] *jarret*
[12] *fesse*
[13] *genou*

high, low, to the left and to the right without leaving its position in any way. With this, being the centre which conducts the sword, it must be placed and held at this height, namely, the pommel of the sword is found at the height of the belt of the leggings[14] and facing the opening of the pocket in order to hold the flank well covered. The wrist, being held in this proportion, makes that it meet itself in a perfect square, namely, between the baseline[15] to that of the belt of the leggings and the pommel of the sword, and the two perpendicular lines which descend one from the guard of the sword to the point of the right foot, and the other behind the point of the shoulder to the ankle of the left foot. Seeing the picture here above labelled A, you will understand the truth of it with a compass.

And for the point of the sword, it should always be presented before its opponent, but for the height of this I will not give any rule here, especially since this depends on the plans that one wants to execute.

The body being thus placed, observing these rules and postures above mentioned, is called being *en garde*, that is to say, fully prepared to attack his opponent or to defend himself from him.

The Parts of the Blade of the Sword and Their Names

To hold the sword in the manner said above, it is necessary to know how to distinguish its parts by their names. The edge which is on the inside towards the fingers is named the true edge of the sword and the other the false edge.

The blade from the guard to the point is measured in three parts of equal length, namely, the part closest to the guard is called the strong; that of the middle, the half-strong; that of the point, the weak.

The weak is used to offend the opponent, the half-strong for engaging the weak of his sword, and the strong for parrying his strikes.

Of the Four Movements of the Body

A man in guard who wants to attack or to defend himself must observe well these four movements of the body, which are firstly to advance; secondly, to retire; thirdly, to bend on the inside very low (when one pushes on *seconde*); and the last [fourth], making a half-turn to the left, turning in an instant on the right heel, followed by two steps

---

[14] *haud de chaussé* - hose, leggings, britches
[15] *la ligne du plant*

withdrawing and closing on his opponent, as I will explain more in its place, which is called to *volte* or to *quarter*.

The movement of the body advancing and withdrawing is made in three different ways, namely, two are made approaching his opponent, one walking[16], the other in narrowing the measure of the foot, and the last by the movement of the body alone, without moving the left foot. This is done pushing these strikes forward, and after returning and putting oneself again in guard, or in leaping backwards in order to break measure.

The movement while walking is made when one is very far from the measure for pushing and giving one's strike to his opponent. In order to do this it is necessary to make these steps walking sideways[17] without departing in any way from the guard and posture. When you see your opponent who desires to fight or defend himself, be it with the sword or the foil, it is necessary that you first draw the sword[18] in the guard and posture outside measure, which is too far removed, and in order to make your approach you will make a step with the left foot, carrying it forward[19] such that the ankle of this is placed directly before the point of the right foot and after you will make a second step with the right foot, carrying it forward too, so that its point is found below and at the level of the guard of your sword, and the heel before and opposite the ankle of the left foot. And thus you will continue your steps until your are close enough to your opponent, but such that you will finish them outside measure from fear that he will take you on the tempo of the foot as you make your last step.

And if also you find yourself too rushed[20], that you are constrained to withdraw yourself in defending yourself, you will be served with the same steps, carrying the right foot behind the left, and the left behind the right, observing always the same distance, proportion and angles in your steps both in advancing and in withdrawing.

The last manner is called "narrowing the measure" which is done after the above-mentioned steps or when one sees oneself close to, not far from, the measure. And in order to do this, it is necessary to lift and advance the right foot forward without bending the knee or jerking the body in any way, then immediately follow it with the left foot, narrowing and drawing it in. And in the same proportion that you advanced the right foot forward, you will follow it with the left

---

[16] *cheminer*

[17] *ces démarches en cheminant de costé*

[18] *mettre l'espée à la main*

[19] *de travers en avant*

[20] *trop pressé*

foot as many times as it will please you until you are in measure,[21] always moving the right foot first without removing the body from the above-mentioned postures. Doing this, you will always have the strength and freedom to attack and defend.

And if your opponent presses you by narrowing the measure, so that you are not rushed and may choose the tempo or the counters more appropriate to him, you will break the measure removing the foot[22] in this way: namely, withdrawing very softly, lifting the left foot and moving it backwards and at the same instant as you will place it, you will land your right foot following it,[23] and thus [you] will continue as many times as you judge beneficial, always moving the left foot backwards first and, in the same proportion that you will have moved it away, you will land the right foot. And in this manner, you will always have the strength and freedom to make such tempos and counters as you please.

Tempo, Same Tempo, Counter-tempo and Counter of the Counter

It is still necessary to explain what the words tempo,[24] same tempo, counter-tempo and counter of the counter[25] mean, since there are several [definitions] which take sable for fox,[26] and some saying they were struck "same tempo" instead of saying "counter-tempo", which is very great ignorance (as you will see) and causes many prickles[27] in our training halls.

These four words are used to discern and distinguish the movements of the body, the wrist, the sword, feet, strikes and parries.

And to start with the first and to make the word "tempo" understood: it is impossible to do any action, however swiftly and nimbly it may be done, without it taking some time to do. For example, one makes a thrust as swiftly and nimbly as one can imagine, to disengage, to parry, to advance, to withdraw: all these cannot be done without taking time. And, thus, that which we call "tempo."

---

[21] *jusqu'à ce que vous ne soyez à mesure*

[22] *en lâchant le pied*

[23] *vous attirerez votre pied droit en l'entrainant*

[24] The word in the original text is *temps* ("time"). However, because we are dealing with "fencing time," I'll use the technical term "tempo" when it aids understanding and "time" in other circumstances.

[25] *temps, même-temps, contretemps, et contre du contre*

[26] *prendre marte pour renard* – mistake one thing for another

[27] *pointilles*

Of Same Tempo

The word tempo names the others that follow since, giving a tempo to you opponent, for example, by throwing a strike at him, is it not true that in the same instant that you thrust against him that he can do the same to you? This happens quite often and it is named "same tempo" because the strikes happen together. And both [fencers] having given,[28] it should be said that they are [both] struck in same tempo and not said in counter-tempo.

Of Counter-tempo

Counter-tempo is named so because of the fact that it is contrary, and the balance[29] to a tempo, and is also the preservative remedy to it. All those who call it counter-tempo when two opponents strike each other, instead of saying same tempo, speak without knowledge of the cause. All the more since he who properly takes a counter-tempo never receives a strike in tempo – which I will show more clearly in the theory of this exercise.

Of the Counter of the Counter

Just as the counter-tempo is opposed to and contrary to a tempo, in the same way, the counter of the counter is opposed to the counter-tempo. The word signifies it sufficiently; that is to say, the contrary to that which is counter-tempo.[30]

And following these rules, we can truly say that there is no man who can boast of having an assured strike because if he takes the counter to his opponent's design, his opponent can nevertheless take the counter to his, and thus one to the other until infinity. But any man who knows how to keep and observe well these rules will always make his opponent fall into his traps if the opponent is less learned than him.

Of the Four Guards

It should be known that all the art and exercise of the sword is founded on four principles or general rules without which there is no clever

---

[28] In period French, fencers "give" and "receive" strikes.

[29] Also, "remedy," "counterweight" or "antidote".

[30] Torturous: *le mot le signifie seulement assez, c'est à dire, le contraire, à celui qui est contraire, au temps*

or clumsy person who can throw or extend any strike which is not one of these four, regardless of the great diversity. The clever person knows how to practice them in order, never making one of them in place of another. The clumsy person uses them by accident without knowledge and most frequently awry. These four rules are named the four guards, namely, *première*, *seconde*, *tierce* and *quarte*.[31] Their names serve to distinguish the thrusts from each other and the postures of the body that one should hold in making them.

Of the Strikes and Thrusts of *Première*

The thrusts of *première* are carried, and plunge, from high to low, namely, having the arm extended and the wrist higher than the head, the point of the sword also being high, the lowering of which, with the movement of the wrist, thus pushes this thrust from high to low. The skilful rarely use this strike since this posture is too perilous, having the body completely uncovered and therefore difficult to preserve. It is called *première* because, in order to use the three others, one must put the sword in the hand, drawing it from the scabbard, being at the side, raising the arm and the wrist high, together with the sword and its point. And when we use it, the opponent should be on his feet in order to pierce him from high to low. It is why all men who draw the sword must do it out of measure from his opponent, among other things, when he sees [the opponent] with his sword drawn before him for fear that [the opponent] will stab him during this tempo.

The Manner of Thrusting in *Quarte* with the Rule to Understand Measure

The strike of *quarte* is extended and pushed in this way: namely, when you see an opening[32] on the inside of your opponent's sword, you will narrow the foot and put yourself into measure. But in order to not be deceived in recognising the true measure in all the strikes you will make, you should know this rule which is infallible: you will narrow the measure until you can touch the half-strong and true edge of your sword to the weak of his, that is, from the middle of your sword to the point, without going out of posture in any way. And when you can touch and engage his sword's weak with the true edge and the

---

[31] First, second, third and fourth

[32] *lorsque vous verrez jour et ouverture* lit. "when you see the day and opening". This is a common redundant phrase throughout the text.

half-strong of yours, you will be at measure and all at once[33] you will push and extend your strike, unbending the left side, extending your arm and bearing the right foot forward, gliding with the strong and true edge of your sword on the weak of his, turning your wrist, so that the fingernails are up and turned towards the sky. And in doing so, you will throw the left arm behind over the hip. And to properly extend and lengthen this strike, the body must have extended forward thus while pushing so that it is in this posture, namely, that the right knee and hips are bent so that the point of the shoulder is advanced in a line from the point of the knee and the knee in a line with the point of the right foot. So that while again putting our perpendicular line again the point of the shoulder, descending, it should touch equally the points of the knee and the foot.

Let the pommel of the sword be at the height of the chin, so that the points of the foot, the knee and the right shoulder follow directly the point of the sword and are covered by its strong and true edge. Let the left side be fully extended and unbent that the heel is held with the whole foot firmly on the ground but lying down and turned on its inside. Let the left shoulder be removed with the arm rearward and covered by the right, that the right hip also be covered by the point of the knee, that the head and neck be held straight and free but thrown a little over the back of the right shoulder, looking and guiding [with] an assured eye, without dazzling[34] the point of your sword in order to adjust it, and strike to the nearest uncovered part that your opponent will present you as if you were shooting a pistol. And although all these postures may be long to write about and to read, this does not prevent them from being done all together and in one instant when making this strike.

With that being well observed, you should not fear that the point of your opponent's sword can touch you, considering that the strong and true edge of yours covers all your body, being in the above-mentioned posture, and chases the weak of your opponent's sword which is before you to push it away and throw it inside so that it is impossible that he can touch you, and likewise when he will also throw at you his strike in *quarte* in the same tempo, you will not touch each other because each strong throws and deflects to the side each weak.

After having extended this strike in *quarte*, you will bring the body back into guard, all at once putting each part of it in the place, shape and figure they were in, always holding yourself well covered with the strong and true edge of your sword, with firmness of wrist, in order to

---

[33] *tout d'un temps*
[34] *brésiller ?*

be ready to parry or take the counter if your opponent strikes you, or strike again and extend another thrust as soon as you see a new clean opening.

Of the Thrust in *Tierce*

The strike of *tierce* is thrown to the outside and above the opponent's sword. You will throw it in this manner: when your opponent will give you an opening on the outside[35] and above his sword. You will narrow the measure in the manner that we have said and as soon as you can touch and engage his sword on the outside with the half-strong and true edge of yours [against] the weak of his, holding the wrist turned so that the fingernails are turned below towards the ground, in this manner you will push in one tempo your thrust in *tierce*, sliding from the strong true edge of your sword to the weak of his in a straight line without raising or lowering the wrist, extending forward the body with all its parts, as we said in making the thrust of *quarte*. There is no difference except that there is no need to remove the shoulder and the left arm or to throw the head on the back of the right shoulder as with that of *quarte*. And instead of having your nails up, you must have them turned towards the earth when throwing this *tierce*. And by doing this, the strong and true edge of your sword produces the same effect and keeps your body as covered and secure as when extending the thrust of *quarte*.

Having extended and thrown your thrust in *tierce* and aptly placed the weak of your sword to the nearest part of your opponent's body, above the guard of his sword, you will retire yourself and put yourself again into guard, holding your arm firmly in front, without any contracting, holding also the half-strong true edge of you sword turned towards the weak of that of your opponent. And whatever disengagement he makes, you should always present your true edge towards his weak, which you can easily do by turning the wrist, in order to hold all the body covered by the strong true edge of your sword and to have the strength and freedom to parry and riposte. This word riposte means to throw a strike after having parried.

Of the Thrust in *Seconde*

The *seconde* is thrown in two ways: from *tierce* to *seconde* and from *quarte* to *seconde*. But both are the same thing, since they are always

---

[35] Fencing lines are imprecisely defined although, usually, all fencing lines refer to the actor rather than the opponent. But not always.

thrown on the inside of the sword and the only a difference is in the disengagement which is made from the outside to the inside which you will do when your opponent will hold his guard high; that is to say, the weak of his sword, being elevated, lowering it to the outside of your right shoulder, showing his flank and underside completely uncovered. You, being in measure, will engage underneath the weak of this sword with the half-strong true edge of yours, having the wrist turned in *tierce*, fingernails towards the ground, and all at once with a movement of the wrist, disengage the weak of your sword from the outside to the inside and thrust below, stretching your body forward, keeping the above-mentioned proportions.

But there is this difference in throwing this thrust of *seconde*. Contrary to the two previous ones, which are thrown from the position of the wrist in a straight line, this *seconde* [is] in an oblique and angled line (which some call a "*caver*") because in throwing it, one carries the wrist as far out as possible to the outside, turning the wrist in this manner so that the thumbnail is turned towards the ground and in this manner making the false edge of your sword turn towards and meet the sword of your opponent. And then you should lower the body as low as possible so that the inside of the point of the right shoulder comes to join (as much as it can) the knee, carrying at the same time the left hand to the ground in order to more easily support it to lower and raise the body, bringing and lowering also the left shoulder in the inside, with the neck and head held on the point of it, looking and following with the eye the point of his sword in order to properly adjust it into the uncovered part and in order to escape [the point] of his opponent.[36] And it is necessary that all these postures are done together and in an instant when pushing this *seconde*, which is thrown, as I said, in an oblique and angular line, because it fits the shape and figure of an angle from the shoulder to the wrist and from the wrist to the point of the sword, and it is necessary that the wrist is held at the height of the shoulder, carrying the points of the foot and knee directly before his opponent and in the same form when pushing other thrusts. See the two perpendicular lines of the second picture. You will find the same distance between them as between the two other postures of *quarte*.

Having thrown this *seconde* in the manner said above, you will return yourself, all in one tempo, into guard, always holding yourself as covered as possible with the strong, true edge of your sword.

The strike of *quarte*-in-*seconde* is the same as the preceding, except that there is no disengagement to make. You will do it in the same

---

[36]Sounds rather like a *passata sotto* or a Spanish vulgar *zambullida*.

tempo as your opponent engages your sword on the inside in *quarte*. At the same instant that he crosses the weak of your sword with the half-strong true edge of his, you will turn the wrist and stretch in *seconde* in the shape and figure that we have descrbed and you will not fail to lower yourself as much as it will be possible for you so that your opponent cannot touch you.

This is nevertheless very difficult for him, in engaging or parrying your weak with his half-strong, since by doing this he removes the point of his sword from you and in this way cannot offend you during the instant that you extend to him this *seconde*. But afterwards, it is appropriate that you are prompt in retiring and putting yourself back in guard or pass by him with the left foot, especially as the strong true edge of your sword does not cover you, nor are you served in any way by this posture.

Here end the description and the true rules that one should know to keep and observe when extending the thrusts of *seconde*, *tierce*, *quarte* and *première*. And whoever does the opposite will overthrow and will destroy all the perfection and surety which can be found within this exercise, which cannot be sought or found in other rules or in fashionable strikes. For it would be to abuse and mock the people and himself, especially as the exercise of the sword alone is at present (though abundant in the majority of men) of such perfection that cannot be found in any other new fashion. Just like crossing a river on a long plank, it is safest is to travel straight ahead like those who have already passed. Anyone who would do otherwise[37] will be in great risk of falling below along with all those who imitate him.

That It Does Not Suffice to Know the Principles Alone

It is not enough to know how to throw and extend in *première*, *seconde*, *tierce* and *quarte*, nor to observe the postures and movements of the body, and generally all that I have written and taught before now. All these are only the principles and foundations that must be fully and necessarily well known in order to achieve the wisdom and knowledge[38] of what is found most subtle in this exercise to put one's plans into action, both in attacking and defending, and to preserve oneself and to keep from falling into the shipwrecks and precipices that one encounters. These are things worthy enough to bid those who want

---

[37] *faire autres démarches*, lit. take other steps
[38] *la science et connaissance*

to make a profession of honour and carry the sword, to spend their time, work and minds there, since the slightest mistake causes the loss of goods, honour, life and often the soul's rest with the families.

Nonetheless, youth was never less curious than today to have some training in this noble exercise. And yet we have never seen as many quarrels, duels, fights and murders as now, in which one of the principal causes is that these youths have no fear or apprehension of that which they have never learned, seen, heard or known, anything which could destroy them forever. This is why, walking like a blind man, they throw themselves recklessly from these precipices, believing them to be but beautiful paths to glory from which they do not know how to withdraw themselves and thus perish there miserably.

For it is a very remarkable thing that the greater number of all those who have the least wisdom and experience in arms are the most quarrelsome, seditious and foolhardy, and who ordinarily fear the dangers the least because (as the proverb says) a knowing man doubts all things an ignorant doubts nothing and finds no difficulty.

So we see every day in our training halls all those who have no other wisdom than a few foundations and principles, who know how to extend the thrust of *quarte*, *tierce* and *seconde*, to parry, to riposte, to do some beats and disengagements of the sword, to also be those who believe themselves as clever, expert and skilful as even the most skilled. Especially since they see all the greatest Masters in this exercise have no other posture, or make their thrusts in any other manner than these, because they do not consider and do not know that this entire science, with its subtleties, is carried out through its foundation and principles, which are *quarte*, *tierce*, *seconde* and *premiere*, and the knowledge of these principles and foundations. But they do not know any of the science which comes after them. And thus not knowing, they behave just like those who walk without light, believing they know the way well and going boldly as if they saw very clearly, getting lost, falling and breaking their necks on some precipice unknown and unforeseen.

Of the Heart Without Skill

But it seems to me that I already hear some of these noble persons who swear on their lives[39] that I account it beautiful, and that there is a difference between the button of a foil and the point of a sword, and that one often sees the unskilled take the advantage over people

---

[39] *qui disent par la mort et par la teste* - literally "who say by death and by the head," an idiom for stating a belief vehmently, or, in idiomatic English, swearing on one's life.

who do marvels with the foil in a training hall, and that one does not observe the sword in the hand at all these times of which I speak, and finally, that there is no need of skill and that it is necessary only to have heart and nobility in order to conquer and overthrow the skilful who have none.

I stand in agreement with them, in that what they call "heart" defeats those who have none, however skilful.

But it is appropriate to know the cause which produces this effect. In order to achieve it, it is necessary to know which part of the body acts, governs and conducts this skill with all the subtlety which is contained in it.

If someone said that it is the "heart," I would say no (although it is this which animates all other parts) and that all men have heart equally according to their measure and that one often sees the smallest beat the greatest and thus it cannot be.

I maintain, therefore, that heart neither guides nor conducts skill in any manner and that it is the eye and the judgement. The eye is the sentinel which uncovers the enemy and the rocks, and gives advice to the pilot (which is the judgement) who, like a good captain, as soon as he is warned gives the order and arranges all his soldiers (which are the members [of the body]), each to his post in order to be fully ready to obey and execute his commands. Yet this judgement is not shared equally in men, neither in quantity nor in quality, some having more of it, others less; some stronger, some weaker; and it is this which causes men to not learn like each other. But he who possesses a good and strong judgement does wonders in the conduct of all that he undertakes.

[Intemperance, Humours, and Judgement]

How intemperance in the four moods of which man's body is composed causes judgement to be lost through the two extremities which are fear and shyness, anger and presumption.

Now [follows the] reason why a man without skill, who is not lacking in heart but rather in judgement, often wins the advantage, sword in hand, over another who would beat a hundred like him in foil, one after the other.

It is because this man, skilful in foil, has neither fear nor apprehension of it, knowing full well that there is no danger and by this means fully possesses his judgement which guides him in this exercise and which makes him perform wonders. But when he realises that he must play well, and that he must draw the sword to defend himself, and when the sentinel comes to tell his pilot and captain that he sees the enemy who arrived armed and furious to fight him, this poor pilot, with this counsel, orders his soldiers to each stick to his duty and prepare to execute his orders. The soldiers, having received this order, prepare themselves to do well. But in doing so, there occurs a quarrel and sedition between four of his rogues who are perpetually making war on each other about who will carry the superiority among them,[40] who come to be stirred up and heated one against the other and then to be mixed, to fight each other, be overthrown and running here and there, by their mutiny putting all their comrades into disorder. The poor pilot may cry out to them, "Calm down. Recover yourselves," but no one obeys. And the more he prays to them and tells them that the enemy is approaching, the more they persist and finally, after having run from all sides they find the door of their poor pilot's chamber open, through which they go inside where they continue their disorder there with such fury that at last this poor pilot is forced to abandon and leave his seat and rudder.

After which, the enemy arriving and boarding this vessel full of disorder and lacking guidance, seeing only a few useless and unused weapons which cannot be used to harm them, it is very easy for them without danger [to make] the Master surrender.

And thus, the cause by which means a man without skill, who does not lack heart or, to say it better, judgement, wins the advantage over the skilful who, on this encounter and occasion, loses heart and judgement by accident, coming from the intemperance and disorder of his four soldiers, the four humours the human body is composed of, which are unequal qualities and contrary to each other, namely, cold and hot, dry and moist. But whoever would want to know more specific reasons should address themselves to the doctors, this being their science, not mine.

But I will say, in conclusion, that these people of heart without skill only boast of such victories, only having won against sick people and those fallen in swoon by the vapours risen from this water, which makes them without movement and incapable of defending themselves. And they wrong and greatly abuse themselves to say that there is no need of skill because it is necessary that they stand in agreement with me, that the art marvellously helps nature and that skill neither destroys nor diminishes at all the heart and nobility of a man. On the contrary, it supports him, guides and strengthens and greatly increases him.

---

[40] *à qui emportera la supériorité l'un de l'autre*

That Anger and Presumption Also Take Away Judgement and Skill From a Man

But I still hear some of these gentlemen who say that it is not only these skills of which we have just spoken that they understand but also those who have shown their skill and courage in numerous combats in which they have won and, after all, it often happens that they are killed by the unskilled.

I agree, but this happens to them by accident, and they perish by another cause completely contrary to that on which we have just spoken, both opposed to each other as two extremes, just like "too much" and "too little." The skill of the first is lost through fear and fright, which proceeds from too great an abundance of the moist and cold humours which, being moved, freeze the heart and the blood in the veins and cause the loss of judgement and render a man without movement and incapable of defending himself. Thus, they [who] lose their skill through anger and fury, which comes from an abundance of blood and bloodiness which produces so great a heat at the least emotion that all the body is filled with fire and flame which sends so much smoke, vanity and presumption into the brain that judgement and all reason is suffocated by it so that a man, only guided by this boiling heat that produces in him fumes of arrogance and contempt, is made clumsy so that he wants to fight for some weak cause of some sort, running precipitously to this fight without order, without fear or apprehension, without thinking of his preservation or considering, like the blind man he is, that the sword of the clumsy pierces as well as his own, and who, seeing himself attacked and in inevitable danger, resorts to playing double or nothing. Making a virtue of necessity, he assembles all his strength and power in the preservation of his person, who, seeing himself reduced to extremity, makes prodigious and almost miraculous efforts in order to extricate himself from everything that bothers him.

All these parts unite and collect with judgement, which also calls to its rescue the sovereign power which is above all human skill, which always assists the right, preserves the innocent and chastises the insolent, and makes [it] that the most skilful and noble person that can be cannot have killed a fly against its will. Moreover, he does not think that he should not play, sword in hand, with an unskilled person who never gives quarter to his opponent when he has the advantage. All the more since there is no fitting or more sure way to get out of danger than to kill him. And in not thinking of all these possibilities, judging the unskilled incapable of hurting him and unworthy of his anger and imagining that he must cut through mountains,[41] and split rocks with a single glance, doing everything filled with anger and fury, thrusting at him, and being extended thus without judgement or guidance, it happens by bad luck that he slides and falls, or his thrust is parried by accident by the unskilled, scrambling with his arm and his sword indiscriminately and like a demon, and having thrown himself bodily from above, he will be pierced and killed miserably, and we will say "Ha!" The weapons are ordinary, there is still a nostalgia[42] and way of speaking, because weapons are always still as capable of offending tomorrow as today, but men are not the same, not being always the same in constitution and willingness to execute their plans from one day to the next,[43] and this further proves that the four elements, by their change, make the man sometimes happy, cheerful, willing, light and vigorous, and another time sad, melancholy, sorrowful, heavy and numb. And therefore, it must be said that men, and not the weapons, are careless and [we may] conclude that these skilful ones perish by accident and by their faults, by letting themselves be carried away by the anger, vanity, arrogance and presumption that disturbs all the senses and the brain, making them lose judgement and all reason, which in this manner makes them much more clumsy than the unskilled themselves. Hence it is not true to say that the unskilled have defeated the skilled, who on this occasion have only the name and not the effect.

However, I advise all those who want to carry the sword, both for the service of the King and to preserve their person, and to repulse force with force, firstly:

To make themselves more skilful in this exercise and to do it devoting time and continual work to it. With full attention, in order to accustom the body to extending, stretching, withdrawing, bending, lowering and retreating with agility, vigour and gracefulness, observing with judgement all the tempos, counter-tempos, and counters of counters, following the order and the manner which I hope to write about below, which would be much easier for me to make understood and to explain with the foil and plastron than through speech and the pen.

Secondly, after having acquired this skill, it must be maintained through exercises with the foil, as often as possible, even if this is only thrusting against a wall in order to train the body and the wrist in their vigour and presence. Whoever fails to do so rusts, becomes numb and weighs himself down in such a way that the most skilled that can be

---

[41] *et s'imaginant qu'il doit trancher les montagnes*
[42] *une vielle rêverie*
[43] *en un jour comme en un autre*

found, even if it has only one or two years without him having exer-
cised at all, will certainly be beaten by a student of six months with the
foil. This is seen quite often. This is why, in order to prevent yourself
from rusting, it is necessary to set on with the foil as often as one can
and to not follow the opinion of some knights of this time who, even
after having done their exercises and being full of themselves,[44] never
want to make an assault with foils in front of people, scared, they say,
of teaching their game and plans to others. But I would believe that
is rather the fear of showing their faults and clumsiness, because it is
necessary to know and understand that nothing can be hidden in the
exercise from a well-skilled man who, through art and experience,
knows how to understand the plans of his adversary and make them
useless to [that adversary] and to use them to his own advantage.

In the third place, take care to not allow yourself to carry to one
or the other of these two extremities of which we have just spoken,
namely, too much fear and terror, or anger, presumption and arrogance, which are the passions which cause great disorder among men,
making them lose all reason and judgement, and in doing so strip them
of all their wisdom and skill, and finally reduce them to the level of
the beasts. And in order to be successful in this practice, it is necessary
to hold oneself in the middle, which is being not too fearful, or too
proud in his courage and skill, waiting (as one says) until mistrust is
the mother of safety and that the sword in the hand seldom makes a
mistake twice.

But holding this middle depends on the gifts of nature and good
constitution, and the proportion of the parts which compose it, with
the guidance of reason.

Also, we see through experience that all those who have been, and
who are there still now, and who are above the common as skilled,
valiant, noble people, they are of good constitution, joyous, ready and
in good humour, who are not fearful or angry, and who one rarely, if
ever, sees fighting over their own quarrel and subject because the skill
that they possess comes to them from the strength and power of their
judgement. And all those who have good and strong judgement do
not do or undertake anything which is without good cause and reason,
and any man who conducts himself through reason and judgement
and wants to do to others that which he wants others to do to him,
[will] by this, never make quarrels.

But, when they have cause to draw the sword against another,
you will see them go there in sober and moderate blood, without pas-

---

[44] *en etant revenu* - Cotgrave carries a sense of "swollen, or puft up"

sion or emotion ever appearing, with as much civility and courtesy as one can make, and fights with the foil with as much judgement and ease as they can, and who gathers more glory and nobility disarming their opponents than killing them. As there are, in effect, many more of them, there are found many who, in all these meetings, content themselves to disarm their opponents without having ever wanted to kill a single one and who even have given their lives to those who gave them a death blow.

We can call these, with just reason, noble and heroic actions. Because there is more grandeur or heart and courage to forgive an offence in this way than to punish it.

It is this which all those who carry the sword and who desire to be thought noble and courageous must imitate in order to employ it in this manner and not do as many young people do who, after an infinity of bragging and impetuosity, from quarrels and swear on their lives, thinking to make the whole earth tremble with fear although they are hardly capable of frightening little children, and who, after everything, tremble with fear themselves before their adversaries when it is necessary to play earnestly,[45] and hot and boiling which they seem at the start, they become at the end cold as marble when their adversaries have the patience to allow them to pass for little their first sallies and endure their words, in which they say "Ha! Head, belly, coward. You lack heart. You drag your foot. You step back," and are answered, "Yes, yes. It is true. But play your game and take care that in the end you do not find it too much for you."

---

[45] *tout de bon*

quarte

B

Seconde

tierce   C   *uolte*

Chapter II

[Theory, Art, and Practice]

In which is treated the theory, the art and exercise of the sword alone or foil, and all that which can be done more subtly with it.

In order to show and make understood what the perfection of play of the sword alone or foil[46] consists of, it is necessary to begin with the parts in order to achieve through each of them knowledge of the whole.

In the first place, it must be known that all the wisdom and subtlety contained in this exercise depends on solidly understanding the movements, tempo, measures, plans and intentions of one's opponent in order to render them useless and use them against him.

But someone could say that it is not possible to recognise and know the plans and intentions of the man.

And I reply that one recognises easily the interior from the exterior and the cause by its effects.

We know the anger and other passions which are locked inside the man by the movements of his members and parts that we see on the outside, be it by his eyes, by his face, by his speech or walk, or by the movement of his arms and hands.

And equally, we know in an instant the plans and intentions of a man who has a sword or foil in his hand, and the information which can be had through the holding of his guard, the situation of his body and sword, and the movements of these.

In order to show this clearly, we must understand all the subtleties contained in this art although the number of them is nearly infinite. Nonetheless, it all works[47] and consists of two points or two parts: where you will attack, and where you will be attacked by your opponent; where you will engage his sword, where he will engage yours; and finally [where] you will thrust[48] him, where he will thrust you.

This being constant and true, I will divide this treatise into two parts. In the first, I will assume that you will attack and engage your opponent and that you are both skilled, and then explain what will be suitable for you and what you should do and observe, both in attacking and defending.

---

[46] *fleuret*

[47] *tout cela roule*

[48] *pousserez*

In the second part, I will flip the coin.[49] Where you were attacking and engaging, you will be attacked and engaged by your opponent, and you will still be taught how you must watch and guard to defend yourself from him, and reverse his designs by carrying out yours.

But before going further, I should ask a question here which will serve greatly in understanding this treatise,[50] which is: how can a man who has a sword in his hand defend himself, being in a training hall[51] in which there are four doors, one before, one behind, one to the right and another to the left, being very certain that his enemy will come through one [door] to attack him in order to kill him but without knowing through which [door he will come]?

I ask what this man must do to prevent his enemy from entering, preserve his life, and to get rid of him.

Someone could say that he would only have to close these four doors and lock them well against him, and leave his enemy outside who can by this means do him no harm.

But this man will remain locked up, prisoner and captive, and cannot not, because of this, extricate himself and defeat his enemy. A better means must be found. Now, here is a very sure method by means of which this man can prevent his enemy from causing him any inconvenience.

It is necessary that this man close and lock well three of the four doors, and afterwards that he guards with his sword that one which he has left open. And when his enemy comes to enter it, it will be easy for him to prevent him and defeat him.

Thus, a man must act in the same manner who has a sword or foil in the hand, who similarly has four doors or openings[52] through which his adversary can throw and give him *bottes*,[53] namely, in *tierce* or *quarte*, or above or below his sword.

This is why it is necessary that the body be held and withdrawn backwards, shortening the left part on its foot, as is represented by our first posture labelled "A", in order to more surely maintain two extremities which would be too difficult to protect if the body were held straight, namely the top and bottom of the sword,[54] in order to more surely close three of four doors and openings with the true edge,

---

[49] *je tournerai la médaille*

[50] *qui servira beaucoup d'intelligence à faire entendre ce traité*

[51] *salle*

[52] *lequel a pareillement quatre portes, ou jours et ouvertures* – repetition removed.

[53] An Italian fencing term for strikes and in particular thrusts. Very common in French texts.

[54] *le dessus et le dessous de l'épée*

strong and half-strong of the sword, and to have the greatest freedom and ease to guard that which one leaves open.

But it is necessary to ensure that in closing your three doors and openings, you restrict also (to be done as one can)[55] the freedom of your adversary's sword in order to force him to fall into your traps.

And in order to do this, and begin our method, we suppose that you are in a large and beautiful room in which you want to attack and set upon your adversary with the foil. After having presented him with two [foils] of proportion and equal length, and having taken and chosen one and leaving you the other, you put yourself at one end of the room, and him in the other end, both directly opposite each other, holding each of the two feet next to each other,[56] the foil in the right hand, the point lowered towards the left side, the two arms held low to the sides without any artifice, after which you will make the salute[57] in this manner.

The Salute[58]

In the first tempo, gently and slightly lift your right foot and move it half a foot away from the left foot and, in placing it down, make sure that the whole body is supported on it and at the same time you will raise your wrist and foil high in first guard or *première*, as you please.

On the second tempo, you will bow with your left foot, putting your left hand to the hat and uncovering yourself, bringing it down next to the knee, turned towards the inside, and it is necessary in making this salute to drag the foot gently by rounding and turning the point of it to the outside, carrying and removing the left side backwards in such a manner that the ankle of the same foot is found behind the right heel, where placing it you will balance your weight[59] so that it is supported by it.

On the third tempo, you will lift your right foot, carrying it and placing it forward, the toes directly facing your opponent.

On the fourth tempo, you will make a step forward with the left foot so that the ankle of this foot is found before the point of the right foot, putting your hat back on your head, and lowering your wrist and foil in *seconde*, without lowering the body.

---

[55] *s'y faire se peut*

[56] *tenant chacun ses deux pieds à côté l'un de l'autre*

[57] *la révérence*

[58] *La révérence*

[59] *vous balancerez votre corps* – the idea of "swinging" like a balance scale doesn't fit here so the additional sense of weighing an object has been used.

And on the fifth tempo, you will make a step forward with the [right?] foot, and you will put yourself in guard and stance in the manner we have previously taught. And it should be noted that in making this salute, you should not lower the head nor bend the body, as in the salutes of politeness that one makes. On the contrary, it is necessary to hold oneself straight in order to look fixedly at your opponent and consider his guard and stance.

Many people make their salute in another manner. But each does as seems good to him because it is only a small ritual which does not do anything to the foundations of this science.

After having made your salute to your opponent, who will have similarly given it to you, and you both being in guard on the fifth tempo, you will narrow the measure gently, considering his guard and posture.

Now you should be certain that no one can hold his guard except in one of the four manners, namely, high or low or in the middle, which is covering himself with the sword, in *quarte* or *tierce*, and it is necessary to not put oneself to pains in this since each is as easy to enter as the others. For in these four different guards, you have to make for each its own [particular] engagement.[60] But you should have a good foot, good eye, good hand, and good judgement with all the required dispositions of the body in order to well execute the tempos, counter-tempos, and counters of the counter with agility, vigour and elegance.

Of the Engagement in *Quarte*

If your adversary holds his guard in the middle and covers himself with his true edge, the strong and half-strong of his sword to the outside, leaving no opening except on the inside of it in *quarte*,[61] you will narrow the measure until you can touch the half-strong and true edge of your sword to the weak of his and, in putting yourself at this measure you will engage the weak of his sword with the strong and true edge of yours, close very well three of your four doors and openings, giving no daylight except to the outside of your sword in *tierce*.[62]

Now, holding the sword of your adversary thus engaged and subjected on the inside, in *quarte*, you should know how to remedy these four things, which are:

---

[60] *vous avez à leur faire à chacune son engagement*

[61] i.e.: the opponent leaves an opening in *quarte*

[62] i.e.: you leave open your *tierce* position

1. Where your opponent disengages and thrusts at you into *tierce*,

2. Where he disengages without thrusting at you, either making a feint or just to free [the sword],

3. Where he will contest against your sword,

4. Where he will not move the point of his [sword], that is to say, where he will remain engaged.

If your opponent takes a tempo to disengage from the inside and push his thrust into *tierce* at you, you will make one of the counters below to him as it pleases you, namely:

1. Where parrying with the strong and true edge of your sword, turning your wrist roundly from *quarte* to *tierce*, bring back in an instant the weak of your sword to the inside (where it was on the outside) holding it a little high in order to better close this opening and turn away and let your opponent's thrust pass by to the outside. This being done, your will riposte and thrust him in *tierce* or *seconde*, if he closes the opening of *tierce*, or in *quarte* if he closes both openings.

2. Where you will parry it with the false edge of your sword (as many people do) and after you will thrust to the body.

3. If he thrusts this strike at you forcing his strong on the weak of your sword so that you cannot turn aside his weak to the outside, you will be served by one of these three counters, namely, the two made by ceding to the force, and the other by turning.

One of the ways to cede to the force is done thus: in the same instant that you feel your weak being forced by the half-strong of your opponent's sword in extending his thrust in *tierce*, you will allow your point to go down and to the inside, softening the wrist, turning and lifting it up in such a manner that the pommel makes the height of your shoulder, your fingernails turned towards your opponent's head. And in this posture, you will find the strong and true edge of the sword on the inside, which will be opposed to the weak of his, which will turn it away and make it pass on the inside without being able to touch you at all, provided that you remove your left side in doing this. And in the instant that this strike is finished, you will lift again the weak of your sword with a movement of the wrist, pushing your riposte in *quarte* at him, where your will not fail to find an opening. This strike is not common, although very excellent.

4. This other manner of ceding, sword in hand, is very good, even against left-handers: it is done almost like the previous, but with this difference. When one thrusts at you in *tierce*, forcing thus as we have just said, you will obey from the wrist, lowering the point of your sword down and lifting the wrist by turning it until the thumbnail is turned towards your knee, the pommel high and to the outside and immediately you will make a turn of your sword in the form of a windmill[63] by turning the movement of the wrist circularly and raising the point from low to high. And in doing this turn, you will not fail to meet the weak of his with the strong of your sword, which will throw it, and it will pass in front of you without it being able to touch you. Finishing the turn of your sword, you could, with a *revers*, give a disarming strike or *estramaçon* with the true edge on the head or the arm of your opponent before he can retire or return to guard and, without which, it would be difficult for him to avoid this strike which, being well applied, which will put him in a state of not being able to do any harm. And if you want to use this strike with the foil, in place of giving an *estramaçon*, it is necessary in completing and finishing your turn of the foil to strike at him and extend the thrust in *quarte* above the strong of his sword. These two ways of ceding to the force are very clean and useful to all those who do not have a strong wrist and will greatly deceive those who throw their thrusts in *tierce*, forcing the strong [against] the weak, because, not finding any resistance [and] instead of adjusting the body, [they] pass very far by across the front.

5. At the same time your opponent throws this thrust in *tierce* at you, turn your wrist into *quarte*, raising it and holding the point of your sword directly opposite his flank below the strong of his sword and, in the same instant, turn and quarter the body by turning on the right heel, a half-turn to the left, making two steps backwards, namely, the first with the left foot, putting the ankle of it behind the right heel, as it is represented in the plate labelled C, and the second with the right foot carrying the point of it behind the ankle of the left foot. And make these two steps sufficiently wide in order to find yourself very close to his right side to prevent him from being able to hit you with the point of his sword through an abbreviated re-taking, and also to prevent him from grabbing you and getting rid of your

---

[63] *moulinet*

sword. You will then promptly make another half-turn to the left, turning towards him, seizing him with your left hand by the back of his thigh.[64] In finishing this, turn and present your sword point at him, in which you will have complete freedom, against his kidneys, from where you can still hit him if you want, which should be done in the case where he wants to try to throw himself on you.

This *volte* or *quarte* is excellent when it is done at the same time as your opponent thrusts in *tierce*. Especially since thrusting it in a straight line with your wrist, you will remove your body from in front of it by doing this *volte*, which by this means he cannot touch you, and you will never fail to give him your thrust in the flank, provided that you turn the wrist well in a *quarte* below his sword and adjust your point as necessary, on which your opponent will not fail to close himself as he will do with his body, by extending and thrusting thus this *tierce*.

6. You can again in the same time that he thrusts you in *tierce*, disengage[65] at the moment he makes his. In throwing his thrust at you, extend yours to him in *quarte*, taking with the strong and true edge of your sword the weak of his own.

7. If your opponent throws his thrust high towards your head,[66] you will parry it by lifting it upwards with the strong and true edge of your sword, breaking the measure backwards with a movement of the body only, lowering it as low as you can, your left shoulder and your head in towards the knee, in order to let this thrust pass above, which being finished, you will bring back, by a movement of the wrist, the point of your sword upwards, riposting and pushing in *seconde*, striking under his wrist.

8. At the same time that your opponent extends his thrust upwards, instead of parrying it, you can throw yours in *seconde*, which is the same counter shown on the plate labelled "B".

9. We have said above that there is much more nobility and honour in disarming an adversary than in killing him. This is why it is

---

[64] *par le derrière de son haut-de-chausse*
[65] *faire un déliement*
[66] Compare this action to Pacheco's *zambullida* and Godinho's *balanzada*. See Tim Rivera's *Iberian Swordplay*, p.140.

very important and necessary to teach the method of it, which is this:[67]

A Very Sure Way of Disarming His Opponent

You can disarm your opponent when he pushes his thrust in *tierce* and he unwinds himself to his full length. You parry it with the strong and true edge of your sword, well closing with it the openings on the outside, both above and below, in order that he cannot touch you with it and, in the instant that this thrust will have passed on the outside, by the opposition of the strong of your sword, you will make a large step forward with the left foot and promptly seize his sword with your left hand, taking it very close to the hilt. In doing this, remove your right side, carrying it behind the left, putting the right foot crooked[68] so that its ankle is opposite your left heel. Present your sword, which you will hold withdrawn to the rear with the point towards his stomach, your wrist turned in *seconde* and held above the right foot, the arms bent in a semicircle. And by this you will keep him subjected by the taking of his sword and the point of yours in such a way that he will have to exchange (as we say at present) and abandon you and leave [you] his sword. Thus, the safest and least perilous manner of disarming of all those which can be done and invented. This same taking is also made as surely [when][69] he thrusts at you in *quarte* as when he thrusts at you in *tierce*.

Second Decision: Of Engagement With a Plan or Without a Plan

I'll move on to the second and say that if your opponent disengages without pushing his thrust at you, you have to understand whether he is doing it with a purpose or not, namely, either to simply disengage his sword or to make a feint, or to give you an opening and compel [you] to strike at him in *tierce* in order to trap you by one of the nine counters of which we have just spoken.

If you fear one of these counters, you will use the counter of the counter which you will make in this manner: in the same instant that he disengages and gives you an opening in *tierce* by doing this, you will push a half-thrust at him to this opening in *tierce* by which you

---

[67] Note that in the original "this" is an emphatic use of the word to point to the section which follows.
[68] *de travers*
[69] *aussi surement qu'*

will see if your opponent has plans to take the counter or not. If he does not move, you will finish your thrust to the body. And if he does strike below at you, or turns the body, believing that you have extended yourself your entire length, you will parry this [thrust] below or this turn [of the body] and then finish with thrusting to the body. And thus, by this counter of the counter, you will take the one who believed he held you. And if he makes this disengagement without the intention of rattling you, you will take him on the tempo of the sword: that is to say, at the time he disengages the weak of his sword from the inside of yours to the outside, you will thrust at him in *tierce*, sliding strongly with the strong on the weak, and doing it thus you will parry and give your thrust together.

Third Decision: About Contesting

If your opponent contests, that is to say, when you engage him with the half-strong of your sword, by this same means closing your three doors in order to guard the one of *tierce*, instead of disengaging and pushing his thrust at you, he wants, by the force of his wrist, to take also with his half-strong the weak of your sword, to reverse it and make you commit to engaging.[70]

To remedy this, you have to yield to force at the same moment that he turns you from engaging to engaged.[71] You will push at him immediately in *seconde* and will pass under him, making a large step forward with the left foot, seizing his sword with the left hand close to the hilt, and disengaging yours from below to above his, which will be done quickly with a movement of the wrist, making it turn in a circle[72] from low to high, passing the point of it in front of your rising right foot and, finishing this turn, presenting it before his stomach. And by this means, you will constrain your opponent to change and make him abandon his sword to you. And if he wanted to make an effort to throw himself on you, you would prevent him from doing it with the point of your sword, with which you can hit him as it seems good to you.

But if your opponent was quicker than you when making your pass and going to seize his sword, he changed [his action] by taking his blade with the left hand above the hilt. As soon as you see this change, you should put yourself in guard again, leaping backwards, fearing that he will hit you with the left hand.

---

[70] *vous faire d'engageant, engagé*

[71] *il vous rend d'engageant engagé*

[72] *rondement*

This means of yielding to the force is very excellent and for two purposes, which are: that by doing it appropriately, you will not fail to hit or disarm your opponent; or do both together.

Fourth Decision: When the Opponent Does Not Move the Point and Remains Engaged

If your opponent does not move and remains engaged, you will push your thrust at him but, before you do so, you need to know these three things, which are:

1. where your opponent will go on to the parry,

2. where he will not go,

3. where he will thrust at you at the same time.

So, to succeed and keep you from falling into these pitfalls, you will act in this way, which is to thrust at him and extend a half-thrust in a *quarte*, extending the arm and the body, bringing the foot halfway forward. In making this half-thrust, you will see in the same tempo his countenance, which will be one of these three things mentioned above.

If he does not make a parry, you will continue and finish making your thrust in *quarte*. Or, if he thrusts at you in the same tempo as your half-thrust, whether by taking the counter from below in *seconde* or by turning, you will use the counter of the counter, which is about parrying this counter, and after you will finish your thrust to the body. If he goes to make a parry, he will do so with or without method.

If he parries with a movement of the wrist, without departing from his position, through the strong and true edge of his sword, which is the best and the most sure, you will thrust at him from *quarte* in *seconde*, that is to say, you will throw this half-thrust in *quarte*, putting all the parts of the body in the same posture as if you had pushed it entirely and at length, on which tempo your opponent will go to close this opening with his aforementioned parry. In the same instant that he touches the weak of your sword, in crossing it with the half-strong and true edge of his, you will turn the wrist and bring all the other parts of the body from the posture of *quarte* into that of *seconde*, and extend and finish this last half-thrust, passing with the left foot and making a grab of his sword in the same manner that we have written about in the third decision of the contest.

Or, if your opponent parries with the strong of his sword by rais-ing his wrist to prevent him from being hit over it, seeing this opening closed, using a movement of your wrist, you will bring the weak of your sword around from above his guard to below where you will find an opening in which you will finish your thrust in *quarte*. This strike is called "to cut in *quarte* under the wrist" or the cutting thrust.

Otherwise, if your opponent goes to parry with all his strength, that is to say, carrying his arm too far to the inside, hoping to chase your thrust far from his body, you will quickly disengage the weak of your sword from the inside to the outside without letting it touch and finish your thrust in *tierce* where you will find there a nice opening which you will take.

And if your opponent is not shaken by your half-thrusts and, when you finish them to your full extent and you cannot touch him because he breaks measure backward with a movement of his body, at this, you will use the *quarte* of the left foot to catch him, which is done in this manner. To better surprise him, you will hold yourself a lit-tle out of measure so that you can push to just touch the weak of the sword to his.[73] And from there, you will throw and extend yourself in *quarte*, extending forward a little more than at the half-thrust and, with a continuation you will complete pushing the body with two steps to reach him[74] and seize his sword, making the first step forward with the left foot, holding yourself always profiled,[75] the left shoulder and arm removed backwards, holding the right arm and wrist well extended to cover yourself firmly with the strong and true edge of your sword. Finally, you will make a second step with the right foot and, in finishing it, you will bring the left side and arm forward, turn-ing them towards your opponent by grabbing his sword. This *quarte* of the left foot is very beautiful and sure when it is done quickly and strikes hard, notwithstanding all the breaks of measure that may be made with movement of the body. It is also excellent against those who parry with the hand, and who are greatly deceived, as you will see it its place.

End of the Engagement on *Quarte*.

---

[73] *en sorte que vous puissiez toucher de votre faible d'épée le sien seulement*
[74] *par deux démarches en le joignant*
[75] *vous tenant toujours bien de côté*

Of the Engagement of *Tierce*

Otherwise, if you see your opponent holds his guard on the inside, not allowing an opening except to the outside of his sword, which we call *tierce*, you will narrow the measure gently and will engage with the true edge and half-strong of your sword the weak of his in *tierce*. Having done this, you must remember the four rules I have determined, which are:

1. where your opponent will disengage thrusting at you in *quarte*,

2. where he will simply disengage, either to feint, or to disengage himself and engage you,[76]

3. where he will contest [the engagement],

4. where he will not move.

First Decision: Disengagement of *Tierce* by Pushing in *Quarte*

If your opponent thrusts at you in *quarte* on the same tempo that you engage him in *tierce*, you should use these counters hereafter in order to preserve yourself and to inconvenience him.

First, you can parry this thrust that he pushes at you in *quarte* with the strong and true edge of your sword, and afterwards you will riposte promptly to the opening which you will see the clearest. But you must understand that there are three different openings which your opponent will allow you by pushing his thrust in *quarte*. But to know which [to use], you have to know all three and have a good and prompt eye to not throw your riposte blindly and at random. And to be sure of the opening you want to give your riposte to, you must consider and watch with a confident eye how your opponent is holding his wrist while pushing his thrust in *quarte* at you. If he is standing high, so as not to leave any opening above this, having parried you will throw your riposte in *quarte* by cutting below his wrist where the opening will be.

If he thrusts in the right line, holding his wrist in the middle in order to not give much opening below it, you will see the opening above the guard of his sword, through which you will thrust your riposte in *quarte*. And finally, if in parrying he carries his wrist too far to the inside in order to chase the weak of your sword with the

---

[76] *et vous engager vous-même*

strong of his, far from his body, allowing by this means all his flank to be uncovered on the outside, having parried with the strong and true edge of your sword, you will push your riposte at him in *quarte* and adjust the weak of the sword crossing on the outside and below the strong of his into his flank that you will find uncovered. This strike is named the *flanconade* because it is given in the flank.

Secondly, you can use this counter here which is very good and sure, which you will do at the same time as your opponent pushes his thrust in *quarte* at you by forcing the weak of your sword with his strong. Without delaying to contest or to parry, at the same moment that he releases his thrust, you will take it by also pushing it at this same moment, yours in *seconde*, lowering your body very low, in order to evade his thrust, which will pass over your shoulder, and you will not fail to give him yours stiffly under his sword. This is the strike presented in plate B.

In the third place, if your opponent in throwing this *quarte* lifts his wrist upwards, in this way leaving his side uncovered at the same time [as] he will let it go, you will evade it by turning and quartering the body, holding straight your sword point to the front of his flank, into which you will not fail to give your thrust.

And finally, if your opponent, pushing you with *quarte*, extends himself[77] with all his strength and length, you can disarm him by using the strong and true edge of your sword, holding the arm and the left side well behind so as not to be touched by this thrust which will pass in front. Which being finished, without removing your true edge from his, you will advance the body forward with this movement, sliding along with the strong of your sword on the weak up to the strong of his, and in an instant turn away the left side and foot, from which you will make a great step forward and promptly lift your sword above his, which will bring the left hand close to his guard, withdrawing yours backwards and presenting the point of it to his stomach and in this way constrain him to change and abandon his sword to you.

Second Decision: Simple Engagement or With a Plan

If[78] your opponent disengages without thrusting but only to release his sword, or make a feint or in order to engage you in *quarte* or to give an opening and cause [you] to thrust at him in *quarte* in order to take the counter from it, whether in thrusting under you or turning the

---

[77] *se débande*

[78] Note that this is not a complete sentence in the original text but somehow must stand with the next sentence in the next paragraph. Weird.

body which are two counters to fear strongly, because it is impossible to do two different actions at the same time (at least regarding those which are these two counters) because one cannot thrust and parry together.

This is why you must use the counter of the counter to remedy this – everything that I have shown you in a similar meeting above in the engagement of *quarte*. If you have to deal with a cunning man who, doing this disengagement purposefully in order to take the counter against you[79] in place of throwing a thrust in *tierce*, you will throw a half-[thrust] on which tempo, if your opponent takes the counter by pushing at you in *seconde* or otherwise turns the body by holding out his sword point in order that you cover it, you will parry this counter with the strong of your sword and then finish and complete your thrust to the body whether in the kidneys, if he turned, or in the side, if he thrust in *seconde*.

If your opponent makes a simple disengagement, that is to say, only disengages his sword, you will thrust at him in *quarte* immediately in the same instant he makes the disengagement, that which is called "taking the time of the sword," or "thrusting on the time of the sword," which is a very beautiful and strong practice. And if he does this disengagement with a beating of the foot,[80] in order to make a show or feint, you could still take [him] on the tempo of the sword. But if you want to catch him in the same tempo that he will make his feint in *quarte*, you will go purposefully to parry in order to give him what he wants, which is the opening in *tierce* to which he will not fail to push his thrust at you. But you must not fail to surprise him there with one of the nine counters which we have written about above in the engagement of *quarte*.

If in disengaging he goes to engage you in *quarte*, you could do two things: either allow him to engage your sword, or not. If you allow him to engage it, in the same tempo that he engages do not fail to cede to the force and push at him in *seconde* with the form that we have said above, or if you do not allow [him] to touch your sword, in the same tempo that he makes his disengagement in order to engage you, you will make a counter disengage, giving him your thrust in *tierce*.

---

[79] *pour vous prendre au contre*
[80] *avec un battement de pied*

Third Decision: The Contest in *Tierce*

If your opponent contests and wants, through the strength of his wrist, to knock away your sword, making himself master of it and keeping you engaged in *tierce*, at this contesting, at the start make a little resistance and at the moment you feel him put all his strength to knock away your sword to the outside, you will disengage the weak and strike him with a thrust in *quarte*.

Fourth Decision: If He Does Not Move

If your opponent endures your engagement and does not move, you must act according to the reasoning that I have written in the same decision on the engagement in *quarte*, which is, that by thrusting in *tierce*, he will either go to the parry or he will not, or he will thrust at you in the same tempo, evading your thrust with his body, whether by lowering it and thrusting in *seconde* or by turning[81] the body. This is why, in order to not let yourself be taken unprepared,[82] you must extend a half-thrust, on which tempo your opponent will not fail to want to carry out his plan. If he takes it underneath, or turns and quarters the body, you will parry, and after, finish throwing your thrust into the opening you find most appropriate in order to strike the body.

If he does not move on the tempo of your half-thrust, you will finish it into the body and if, by finishing it on the firm foot and extending to your entire length, he breaks the measure by a backwards movement of the body such that you cannot touch him, instead of finishing on the firm foot, you will finish by making a passing step towards him with the left foot. If he goes to parry, this will be by raising this strike upwards with the strong and true edge of his sword, lowering the body and the head, or he will parry to the outside, either with the true edge or the false edge of his sword. If it is by raising and lifting, you will finish your thrust by cutting under the wrist in *seconde*.

If he goes to parry in *tierce* with the strong and true edge of his sword, you will finish your thrust by disengaging and thrusting in *quarte*.

And finally, if he goes to parry with the false edge of his sword, you will turn the wrist from *tierce* into *quarte* and complete pushing your thrust to the body, turning and closing on[83] your opponent, be-

---

[81] *en voltant*

[82] *ne vous laisser prendre sans vert*. The 1694 *Dictionnaire de l'Académie Française* gives an option for *vert/verd* as "Qui n'est pas encore dans la maturité requise."

[83] *joignant*

ing careful that he does not strike you on the inside, which remains uncovered.

And the reason why it is necessary to finish this thrust from *tierce* in *quarte*, it is because all those who parry with the false edge, remove the sword point from in front of their opponent and allow an opening in doing this to the outside above the wrist through which we can strike them in the body by thrusting in the aforementioned manner.

Third Engagement: Of the High Guard

If your opponent holds his guard high in order to not allow his sword to be engaged and to have greater freedom and strength to execute his plans.

Notwithstanding all this, appearing to threaten the sky with his sword, he should not put you to trouble. In order to make his guard and execution of this useless, you will close your doors and openings closest and most convenient to this enemy and leave him the furthest opening in which you will confidently await. And to do this, you will attack and engage this high guard from below with the half-strong and true edge of your sword, which you will hold firmly with the hilt sloping and crossing so that the point of your sword is raised a little upwards in order to not allow any opening above it by which your opponent can hit you. This is why you should hold your body withdrawn backwards on the left side, holding the shoulder and the head leaning a little to the inside towards the knee, and in this order you will narrow your foot until you are in measure and whenever you can touch with your sword the weak of his, it does not matter to you, sufficing to lock it up from above and make it impossible [for him] to be able to touch you, being covered there as was said, not giving any opening except below your wrist, which opening you will guard carefully to prevent your enemy from entering there. And in order to do this, you must observe the same command that we wrote about in the preceding engagements, which is that, holding it thus engaged from below and closed above your sword, he will not be able to do anything else other than to disengage, thrusting at you in *seconde*, or he will disengage simply or with a plan, or he will contest, or he will not move.

If he thrusts at you in *seconde* by disengaging from above to below, you can parry this strike in three different ways, namely, first with the strong and true edge of your sword, leaving the point of it above, and with a movement of the wrist throw this strike to the inside in order to make it pass in front of you without touching you; second, parry it with the half-strong and true edge of your sword, as if giving a whip strike by turning your point from high to low, lifting your wrist high and turning it in this manner so that the fingernails are towards your opponent's head, and in this manner, again, you will throw this thrust to the inside in front of you; or third, you will parry with the true edge of your sword, lowering the point of it downwards and turning your wrist into *seconde*, which will prevent your opponent's disengagement and will make his thrust pass to the outside without touching you. And after having done one of these three parries, you will riposte and push your thrust into the best opening that he will present to you.

You could also do this same thrust, this counter, which is very subtle but it is necessary to have a very lively and quick body. In the tempo that your opponent will make his disengagement in order to throw his thrust in *seconde*, you will take it on the tempo of this disengagement, thrusting at him in *quarte*, turning the body and, being done, you will not fail to give yours and render his ineffective. And every time that one makes this disengagement at you, whether to thrust at you or to feint, you can do the same counter.

If your opponent contests with his sword against yours and goes to pass over you and seize you, you can take it on the tempo of the foot, that is to say, at the same instant as he will lift the foot in order to advance on you, you will thrust at him in *seconde* by disengaging from high to low.

If he does not move and stands engaged with the intention of obliging you to thrust at him in *seconde* in order to take you on the counter tempo, to render all of his plans useless, you will make a feint[84] below with a half-thrust, on which, if he thrusts at you in *quarte* and turning the body (as I just said), you will use the counter of the counter, either by counter-turning or parrying.

This thrust can be parried in two ways. First, raise the weak of your sword and quickly close this door that you have allowed open in making the feint, and by this means you will make this thrust pass above you shoulder without doing any harm, and after, you will riposte at him and give your thrust to the kidneys if he has extended while making a *quarte*.[85] Second, parry by ceding to the strength (in the manner that we have described at the start of the engagement in *quarte* when one thrusts in *tierce* forcing the weak with the strong) turning the sword from low to high and finishing this turn, give a with a *revers* a cut to the head.[86]

---

[84] *une demonstration*

[85] *en quartant* (lit.) in quartering, another term Besnard uses for the *volte*

[86] *donner d'un revers un coup d'estramaçon*

Or else, you will do the counter-turn to his, which is very excellent in this encounter and which you will use at the same time that your opponent will thrust at you in *quarte*, on the same tempo as your half-thrust, turning the body or on the firm foot, you will also turn in order to remove your stomach from before his thrust and, in doing this, turn the wrist into *quarte*, holding straight and firmly the point of your sword directly before his kidneys, which will not fail to meet them in joining one to the other while retiring, and thus you will evade his thrust by giving yours.

And finally, if your opponent is rattled and goes to parry your half-thrust, you will take it in the tempo of his rattling, pushing your sword in *tierce* at him.

And if he is not rattled and does not move in the tempo of your half-thrust, you will continue it and finish immediately into the body in *seconde*, either on the firm foot or passing, as will seem good to you.

Fourth and Last Engagement: Of the Low Guard

If your opponent holds his guard low, namely, the point of the sword towards and near the ground (either with his wrist turned in *quarte* or in *tierce*), this does not present you with all of his body uncovered above his sword. You must believe that he is not doing this without a plan and judge what that could be.

Now, his plan will unfailingly be to give you the desire to extend your thrust to this body that he is holding out uncovered in order that, on this tempo, he can take you with a counter, which will be either to parry with the hand (as is ordinary with all these holders of similar guards) or to turn or to take from below or, if you go first to beat his sword to take the counter, defying the weak of it and thrusting at you above yours.

In order to deceive the deceiver, and to escape all his ambushes, you will put yourself in measure and engage this sword from above with the true edge and half-strong of yours, with which you will close securely your openings below, [and] have no openings above these to guard. And if your opponent takes the counter of your engagement by disengaging from below, thrusting at you to your opening, do not fail to take the counter of his counter, namely, either to parry, lifting this strike upwards, and afterwards riposting to him cutting under his wrist in *seconde*, or evading his thrust by turning the body, turning the wrist in *quarte*, and inclining towards him and presenting the point of your sword straight and firmly in front towards his body (as is represented in Plate C) or to thrust from below in *seconde* at the tempo he thrusts at you from above.

Otherwise, if he does not move and stands engaged, presenting his left hand forward to parry, push at him with a half-thrust on which, if he thrusts at you from below or turning, you will parry this counter and then finish your thrust to the body where, if he does not move and is not shaken by your demonstration, you will complete it to the body.

And if he is shaken and goes to parry with his hand from high to low, you will suddenly disengage the weak of your sword, turning it away with a movement of your wrist from below [to] above his hand and finish your thrust, whether on the firm foot or passing by him with the left foot.

Or, if he is not shaken, standing assured before completing, you will make a beat of your sword and then push to his body, deceiving his hand and his sword, with all his plans, in executing yours.

That the Hand Parry is Dangerous

The hand parry is very dangerous to those who use it because they must present all of the body's front to their opponent and in consequence [it is] very difficult to preserve [it]. Besides, it is much easier to deceive the hand than the sword. And in this posture, the body is not free to dodge, nor execute tempos, counter-tempos and counters of the counter, and ultimately can have no other purpose than to parry and riposte, which isn't much, understanding that the best counters are done without parrying. This is why, having seen and considered what was absolutely necessary, we abandoned the daggers, having found that the parry with the strong of the sword and avoiding [thrusts] with body were much more excellent and sure than parrying with the hand and the dagger, which were deceived every time.

Here is the very sure method which you must hold, keep and observe in attacking and engaging your opponent, either with sharp swords or foils.[87] This method consists in two things, theory and practice. And anyone who can possess them, bind and join [them] together, through good conduct and strength of judgement, will work wonders in this exercise. But possessing and joining these two parts cannot be done without spending a lot of time and continuous work on it.

---

[87] *avec l'épée blanche ou fleuret*

Objection

But [what] if someone said that I put all the perfection of this sword exercise in the engagement of it, even though many people have their wrists so subtle in the disengagement that it is impossible to hold them engaged or even touch their sword?

To this I respond with my proposal in which I said that by closing your three doors and openings, it is also necessary in doing so to lock up (if it were possible) the freedom of your opponent's sword and to guard well the fourth door that you would leave open, and then I showed you, in all the tempos, movements and disengages that he could have made at you, all the remedies and counters necessary to preserve you and to defend yourself from him.

And it must be understood, when I spoke of locking up and engaging the freedom of your opponent's sword, that it is absolutely not necessary to touch it with yours because I know very well that this cannot be done with all people, each holding their guards differently: some hold them withdrawn, others very high or low, and a few across and so far to the inside or outside that it is impossible to touch them.

But this does not prevent you from closing your doors which are closest to your enemy and that you only expect [an attack] at the one that you leave open, which by this means locks him out and removes his traps, and breaks all his plans, making him fall into and be caught in yours.

However, before moving on to the second part of this treatise, I must speak of the retakings,[88] feints and beatings of the sword.

Of Retaking

Retakings are very excellent and necessary in this play and exercise of the sword and are done in this way (for example). If I see that my opponent gives me an opening in the *quarte*, into which I push a thrust at him, and on the tempo he goes to the parry and closes this opening with the strong and true edge of his sword, dropping his foot back to break the measure, at the same time,[89] I will drag my left foot and in bringing it close to the right heel, disengaging my sword point from inside to above his, I will thrust at him in *tierce* and, if he goes again to parry it and raise it up, I will disengage from above and thrust below in *seconde*. And finally, if he goes to parry it again below, I will disengage below his sword by pushing on it and so, while he continues to parry,

---

[88] *reprises*
[89] *tout d'un temps*

I will also continue to push and extend my thrust to the openings that he will give me until I catch him and strike him. And thus, this is what we call retaking.

Of Feints or Demonstrations

Feints and demonstrations are the same thing. There are four different guards, which cause four engagements; four engagements, four lights and openings; four openings, four disengagements; the four disengagements, four parries; and the four parries, four feints.

Feints serve to deceive parries. Feints are dangerous to the one who does them if he does not know how to perform them,[90] support and defend them with counters, for whoever does them with no other plan than to rattle his opponent is soon taken in the tempo of his demonstration.

But in order to use them confidently, here is how you should act. For example, you see that your opponent is properly in guard and covered, that he only gives you an opening in *tierce*, which he gives you as a trap designed to take you if you go there recklessly.

So to remedy all inconveniences which could happen to you, you will make a demonstration of throwing your thrust into the opening of *tierce*. But before doing this, you should be very assured whether your opponent will go to parry or will not, or will push at you in the same tempo as your feint. If he goes to parry, you will take him in his confusion,[91] finishing your thrust at him in *quarte*. If he does not go to parry, you will continue your thrust and finish it straight in *tierce*, and if he pushes in *tierce* in the tempo of your feint, you will take it by one of the nine counters written of in the first decision of the engagement in *quarte*.

Feints by half-thrusts are greatly demonstrative and deceive many because they are very close to full thrusts, which force a man to uncover his plans which, being discovered, cannot serve him other than for his loss. They are made with the movement of the wrist in *tierce*, in *quarte*, above and below the sword and must in no way withdraw the arm when making them. We can make simple, double and triple [feints].

---

[90] *s'il ne sait les suppléer*
[91] *sur cet ébranlement*

Of Beats With the Sword

Beating the sword is very good and it is done with a movement of the wrist, hitting first the weak of the sword with the half-strong true edge. But whoever wants to use it should similarly use the same precautions that I have just shown and taught above in the section on feints, since a man with good judgement[92] must never do or undertake any action before having thought through or foreseen all the events which could happen there.

These beats greatly serve a man with a good and lively wrist, beating with a movement of it, with true edge and half-strong of his sword, the weak of that of his opponent in order to make an opening, pursuing the weak of the sword in front of him, wearying [the opponent's] wrist and interrupting his plans.

But since there is no great wrong, there is no remedy. All the same, you cannot execute any tempo to which one cannot make a counter.[93]

This is why, before making this beat, you must be assured that your opponent will allow beating his sword, and then he will parry or will not, or take the counter of your beat in disengaging and pushing his thrust at you. For example, if you want to beat your opponent's sword in *quarte*, you need a tempo in order to do this in which he could take the counter, which is the most beautiful and subtle that can be executed, namely, that at the same time that you go to beat his sword, he disengages his point subtly without allowing you to touch it and thrusts at you in *tierce*, where he will not fail to hit you if you are not fully prepared to do the counter of the counter, which you will do in the tempo that you see your beat ineffective. And [when] your opponent thrusts at you in *tierce*, you will turn the body, turning the wrist into *quarte* holding the point of your sword straight and firmly towards his flank. And in doing so, you will evade his thrust by slipping the body aside and removing it from above his line and you will not fail to adjust yours and, by this means, if his counter is good and subtle, your counter to his counter will be more so, which is like giving a remedy to an incurable disease.

If your opponent allows you to beat his sword and does not parry promptly, you will thrust at him in *quarte*, and if, after your beat, he closes promptly his opening in *quarte* with his parry, you will disen-

---

[92] *vn homme bien sensé*

[93] *Mais comme il n'y a pas grand mal, qui n'y ait remèdes ; tout de même vous ne sauriez exécuter aucun temps que l'on ne vous en puisse faire le contre.* I believe I have the sense of this sentence correct.

gage thrusting at him in *tierce*.

The beats are made in *quarte* and *tierce* above and below the sword.

End of the First Part

Second Part

Where it treats of how a man must defend himself against his opponent who attacks him and engages his sword.

Following my promise, I have shown and taught you, in the first part of this treatise, the method and manner of acting which you must hold, guard and observe when attacking and engaging your opponent. And in this second part, I flip the coin to make you see and understand how you must defend yourself from a man who attacks you and engages your sword.

First Decision of the Engagement of *Quarte*

1. Let's suppose again that after you have come on guard that your opponent comes to attack you, who having narrowed the measure, engages your sword on the inside in *quarte* with the half-strong and true edge of his, holding himself so well covered that he leaves no opening other than on his sword in *tierce*.

Being thus, it is necessary that you know that what you can do to another, he can do the same to you and that he gives you no opening without taking care to guard it well and catch your there.

But, as they say, in the end it must be an end-and-a-half[94] and without hurrying or rushing because there is only the desire to give (in this play) that which you receive. If you see that your opponent narrows the measure against you so quickly that he does not give you the leisure to form a plan, you will break the measure from him by withdrawing the foot, as many times as you please and until you have recognised his plan and until you have chosen your time to counter him.

If he narrows the measure with you with haste, running at you, you will foresee it and take [it] on the tempo of the foot and will yield to the force, pushing your thrust in *seconde* at him and then, passing with the left foot at him, you will seize his sword with your left hand very close to his hilt, disengaging and presenting the point of yours in front of his stomach in order to constrain him to abandon his to you, and to mock him.[95]

---

[94] *à fin il faut être fin et demi* – an expression meaning absolutely complete or "done done" in modern Australian business parlance.

[95] The 1694 edition of the *Dictionnaire de l'Adacémie Française* adds this sense to *chanter*: *On dit prov. & fig. à un homme qui dit quelque chose, qu'on n'approuve pas, qu'on ne trouve pas à propos, C'est bien chanté. Mais cela ne se dit que par moquerie.* It's really the only option I have to make sense of this phrase.

This strike is very excellent and sure in this engagement because, as I have already said above, it is impossible to do two things at once and at the same time, as it is to walk and push his thrust because it takes two tempos to do these two things. This is why there are many people who use this ruse, who release the foot expressly to take their opponents on the tempo that they carry themselves forward in order to put themselves into measure and, by consequence, all those who run at their opponents, believing to frighten them and give their strikes, also run greats risk and peril since all men who know how to anticipate them in this tempo will not miss them.

2. And if your opponent, narrowing the measure, holds himself in good strength and position, you will make a feint, subtly disengaging by a movement of your wrist from the inside, pushing at him a half-thrust in *tierce*, gliding with the half-strong of your sword on the half-strong of his in order to see his plan in this instant, which will be wanting to execute one of the nine counters mentioned above or hereafter.

If he goes to throw his thrust below and by turning, you will parry this counter and then finish your thrust to the opening that you will find most convenient.

3. If he does not move on the tempo of your half-thrust, you will finish it directly in *tierce*.

4. If you throw your half-thrust at him, forcing your half-strong to the weak of his sword, he will parry in order to lift this strike upwards. You will finish your strike cutting under his wrist in *seconde*.

5. If he goes to parry and turn away your strike to the outside with the false edge of the sword, you will finish your strike from *tierce* into *quarte*,[96] pushing it over his wrist, turning the body, while making two steps backwards.

6. If he goes to parry with the strong and true edge of his sword to close his opening in *tierce* by this, you will make at this tempo a disengagement and finish your thrust at him in *quarte*.

7. If he breaks the measure with a movement of his body in order to prevent you from touching him, instead of finishing on the firm foot, you will finish by passing with the left foot.

---

[96] *de tierce en quarte*

8. Otherwise, if you see that your opponent is entirely devoted to parrying and riposting, keeping you engaged and giving you an express opening in *tierce* in order to invite you to push your thrust, with the intention of parrying it in order to trap you in the riposte, whether he parries with his sword or with his hand, it doesn't matter which (and this could be a dagger) you can satisfy him in spirit and do that which he desires in order to take him with the same trap that he holds out for you. And in order to do this, you must, in disengaging, thrust at him in the same tempo in *tierce* and allow him to parry it. But you must be quick to come back on guard, allowing yourself expressly to leave an opening on your sword in *tierce*. To this end, seeing only this opening, he pushes his riposte there for which you will be well prepared to take the counter, either by thrusting below, or by turning the body, or another of the above-mentioned nine counters as pleases you, and so you will deceive the deceiver. Thus, an excellent means of trapping those who parry[97] with the hand and dagger, especially as when pushing the ripostes they must leave the dagger and the hand behind, ensuring that it cannot prevent them from receiving this counter.

9. You can also use this manner of doing [things], namely, remaining engaged without moving in order to give the opportunity to your opponent of pushing his thrust at you in *quarte*, on which tempo you will take it with one of these counters, which are either to parry with your sword and after to riposte;

10. Or otherwise without delaying to parry[98], on the tempo that he pushes at you in *quarte*, to throw your strike at him below in *seconde*;

11. Or turning and quartering the body;

12. Or disarming him in the manner that I have previously taught in the first part of this treatise.

13. And if he made a demonstration of thrusting at you in *quarte* in order to sound out your plan, you should still give him this satisfaction, which is that on the tempo of his feint, whether he does it with a half-thrust or otherwise, you will go with a premeditated plan to parry, opening the door of *tierce*, closing that

---

[97] *les pareurs*, (lit) the parry-ers
[98] *sans vous amuser à parer*

of *quarte* and, as it is certain that he will not fail to make a disengagement on this tempo in pushing this thrust in *tierce*, where you will have expressly allowed him the opening in which you will not fail to take him with one of the nine counters mentioned above.

14. Or, on the tempo that he goes to engage your sword in *quarte*, you will make a simple disengagement without thrusting and if he takes this tempo of the sword and pushes his thrust in *tierce* at you, do not fail to do again one of the nine counters to him.

I believe thus there are enough counters and subtleties on this engagement which can all be carried out easily provided that they are practised through long and continual work.

Second Decision: Of the Engagement of *Tierce*

If your opponent, attacking you, engages your sword in *tierce*, you must observe the same method as we did above:

Firstly, being engaged, you will take care to guard well your door and opening in *tierce*, in which every time your opponent pushes his thrusts there, be well prepared[99] to receive it there and take it with one of the nine counters above-mentioned.

But if he is wary of it and does not thrust at you, keeping you engaged in *tierce* in order to constrain you to disengage and thrust at him in *quarte*, where he gives you an opening in order to take you with a counter, to evade his traps and have him fall into yours, you will push at him a half-thrust, disengaging from *tierce* into *quarte*, gliding firmly with the half-strong and true edge to the weak of his sword. And if he thrusts on this tempo underneath or by turning, you will parry this counter with the strong of your sword and, after, you will finish your strike to the body in the opening that he will present.

And if he doesn't move, you will continue and finish your strike in *quarte* above the guard of his sword or, if he goes to parry with the strong of his sword by raising his wrist, you will finish your strike in *quarte*, cutting under it.

Otherwise, if he goes to parry, crossing with his half-strong the weak of your sword, you will finish with *quarte* in *seconde*.[100]

And if he goes to parry with all his strength, carrying his wrist too far to the inside, you will finish disengaging your point in *tierce*.

---

[99] *tenez-vous bien préparé*
[100] *de quarte en seconde*. This sounds very much like the modern *sixte* position.

And if he breaks measure on the tempo of your half-thrust in *quarte*, instead of finishing on the firm foot, you will finish doing the *quarte*, passing with the left foot.

And again if your opponent becomes fond of the parry and riposte, you must give him what he wants: give him the hook that you will present to him. To bait [him], you will push at him immediately on the tempo, disengaging and striking in *quarte* with the plan that he will parry, and afterwards you will put yourself promptly into guard, breaking the measure backwards with the movement of the body only, and in breaking it you will allow an opening in *quarte* above the guard of your sword into which opening your opponent, having parried, will not fail to throw his riposte in *quarte*. And on the instant that he releases it, you will anticipate it with a retaking that you will do to him pushing in *seconde*, lowering your body as low as you can in order to evade his thrust and give yours.

Or in this manner, which is that pushing him in *quarte*, you will carry the wrist a little high and to the inside, and breaking the measure backwards in this posture, you will allow your entire flank [to be] uncovered on the outside of your sword in order to oblige him the throw at you there the strike of the *flanconade*, which then pushing you with his parry in this opening which you have left open on purpose and in the same instant that he releases this riposte, you will anticipate it with the retaking that you will do to him, turning your wrist from *quarte* to *seconde*, which will close this opening, will parry his riposte and will make it pass to the outside and in the same tempo you will extend [your sword] to him in *seconde*.

Of the Two Remaining Guards, Namely, the High and the Low

As for the high guard and the low guard, they depend on the will: either one will do [them] and hold them, or one will not. You could use them sometimes to thwart and interrupt your opponent's plans and in making them, observe the same diligence, precautions and subtleties that we have described and taught in the decisions of the two preceding guards, which there is no need to repeat for these last two especially since it would be more boring than necessary, warning you never to make any tempo or movement of the sword or body, ineffective or in jest, being in front of your opponent and in measure without knowing why, with what intention, or anticipating what which could happen to you, in order to guard against anything which could inconvenience you.

How One Must Act Against Those Who Circle Around Their Opponents

If you have business with an opponent who does not stand firm before you and, on the contrary, always stands out of measure, running, leaping and gamboling sometimes forward, sometimes backwards, making a thousand pantomimes[101] and postures, with the intention of tempting you to run at him or to confuse you and surprise you, imitating those birds which circle, land, beat their wings for a long time above a field mouse with the plan of putting it to sleep in order to take it afterwards, do not worry about all that. Take care only to close well three of the four doors and guard that which you will leave open, and always turn your body in front of him in proportion as he turns around you. And also, make like a cat, which does not move and seems to sleep when it sees a mouse dallying around it and, as soon as it approaches too close, it leaps suddenly[102] on it and takes it.

Equally, if your opponent, after having done his antics believing to have put you to sleep through this, goes running and leaping to extend his thrust to you, do not fail to take the counter where you expect him and foreseeing it on the tempo of the foot.

And if the same opponent, in making his antics, makes a demonstration of throwing his thrust at you to the opening which you will give him in order to make you parry, do not fail to serve him according to his desire and go to the parry, closing this door and this opening properly. For example, give an opening in *quarte* to which he makes his feint, on which you will go to the parry and, closing this opening of *quarte*, you will take him from there with one of our nine counters.

Against Those Who Hold Their Swords With Two Hands

Sometimes people are met who, putting themselves into guard, hold their swords with two hands, taking the blade in one of them above the guard, a posture greatly perilous to him who uses it, especially since it presents the body directly in front of his opponent and can have no other plan and subtlety to execute than to parry or beat his sword and afterwards thrust at him, which is so little that it does not warrant putting oneself into such great risk and danger because, as a parry, it can never be done so well with two hands that there is not

---

[101] *pantalonnades*
[102] *tout en un instant*

sufficient of an opening inside or outside near the wrist in order to give your thrust through it to the body, and then there is nothing so easy as to deceive this one either by simple or double feints. Besides, it is very easy to disturb that hand which is advanced towards you with which he holds the blade of his sword, whether by piercing it with the point of yours or cutting its fingers with its sharp and true edge, hitting with a movement of the wrist, sliding all the way along his blade. Or, if he wants to beat your sword and make the peasant's strike[103] at you, be fully prepared on the tempo of his beat to take the counter by disengaging [and] thrusting him in the body.

Finally, to put it bluntly, this guard and posture is worth nothing at all, being too risky and perilous, among other things, to the sword, if it were not against some clumsy person who would have the wrist very strong and advanced forward, who could not make any disengagement of the sword. In this case, this peasant strike could serve you greatly, subtly beating and diverting this tip from in front of you with the force of both hands and afterwards thrusting it to the body. But the only thing to be careful of with this posture and sword-holding is to not let it touch or beat yours in any way. And if it happens (as it can be done) that your opponent makes a beat at you, make in the same instant a leap backwards in order to prevent him, after having beaten your sword, from hitting your body, which you must not fail to do in all other and similar encounters which could happen to you, where your plans will be interrupted, in order to do them again and prevent the execution of his own.

In order to not be too boring, I have cut away and abridged again here many things that I would have and could have explained in this treatise. But if I undertook to compound all that could be done and executed in this art and exercise, I would throw the reader into a labyrinth in which confusion would bring him more annoyance than satisfaction. This is why, for fear of being too long, I will not go further and will finish here this treatise on the theory and practice of the art and exercise of the sword and foil, in which I have taught and explained more clearly than it has been possible for me all the principle parts, subtleties and tricks necessary in order to have and possess knowledge of the whole and of acquiring the skill of handling the sword well.

This method can be practised sufficiently well left-handed against the left-handed, right-handed against the left-handed, left-handed against the right-handed as the right-handed do against the right-

---

[103] *la botte de paysan*

handed, being entirely the same method of doing and acting except that there is this difference that must be observed when one pushes one's thrusts against a left-hander, namely, of pushing *tierce* to the inside of his sword and on the outside of it thrusting in *quarte* in order to slide with the strong and true edge of the sword on the weak of his.

There are also the strikes in *seconde*, which are very different against a left-hander than the ones right-handers push against right-handers. Besides, [there are] a number of other things that I could resolve which are not common or usual between the right-handed and the left-handed. But, in order to not be too unwelcome and to not engage myself to make a long discourse on this subject, I will content myself at present with what I have here above treated being sufficient only to lead and guide all sorts of minds to a full knowledge of all that concerns this art, for the perfection of which it will remain only a little exercise, both to strengthen the wrist and to experience the lessons which I have given in this book, as sure as that are evident. Enjoy, therefore (very dear reader) and read them with as much care as I present them to you with affection.

Chapter III

Where One Shows the Inconveniences of Combat With Handguns, Short Swords on Foot

Objection

But some moralists and magistrates could say to me, "Who moves and invites you to put down in writing the art and the subtleties in order to show and teach men the means of killing each other? Do you not know that single combat and duels are forbidden by divine and human laws and are punishable by death and ignominious tortures? You and all those who demonstrate this exercise are the fundamental cause of all these misfortunes and disorders because this skill invites and pushes those who possess it to put it into practice at the slightest opportunity and thus you show the path by which you send (with skill) some to hell and others to the gibbet."

Reply

To which I respond, and will show hereafter, that it is not at all our teaching or the skill which causes and invites men to destroy one another in such unhappy ways. My intention is far removed from teaching them this way; on the contrary, all that I have written in this little treatise is only for giving light and clarity to those who have none, in order for them see and understand these unhappy reefs, shipwrecks and precipices, the difficulty that there is in getting out of them, the way to retire from them, preventing all those who have eyes and judgement from putting themselves there, and teaching them to preserve and defend their lives and goods against those who would take these from them – which is permitted by natural and divine laws.

And it must not be said that it is the skill which leads men into these fatal combats. For it is seen daily (as I have already said here above) that the most ignorant in the exercises are those who, through their recklessness and blindness, throw themselves most often into these labyrinths of misfortune and who attract to them the skillful whom they take for seconds to support their follies, cowardice and ill-founded quarrels.

And to demonstrate the contrary, I say and show that ignorance is very wicked and pernicious in this exercise, as well as in all other sciences, because is it not ignorance which has recently brought the

fashion and the introduction of a new fight which is, without comparison, more detestable, abominable and horrible than all those of
whom we have ever heard: the pistol and short sword on foot that the
demon, rage and despair, have invented and put in the heads of the
desperate and angry with nothing to do. [These people,] not having
wanted to undertake the work, or not having the patience to give sufficient time to acquire the skill of wielding their swords (which they
carry unworthily by their side, and who, tickle each other in their
idleness and slothfulness) hate this work as a great torment and, hot
and cold, they always serve as excuses and exemptions from showing
their ignorance in front of the world. They, finally knowing themselves weak on this side, force their adversaries (whom they know to
be more skilful than them) to fight with the handgun and the knife on
foot at the doublet or the shirt,[104] or presenting to each other the chest
of his doublet and firing directly at each other and hitting each other,
and by these terrible and violent blows lose judgement, but still each
of them having the sword in the hand, nature makes a second effort
to support itself and to play with its remnant and to emerge from this
last peril and to get rid of its enemy. And although both are astonished
and stunned by death blows, which they gave each other in the heart,
they still throw themselves on each other, passing [the swords] right
through the body and in this way they immediately vomit everything
onto the field [and] their souls into hell.

Is this a good fight which earns those who do it, and are its authors,
as much honour, praise and glory as those who hang themselves, who
drown and who throw themselves at each other in rage and despair?
And which will bring much profit to the demons, who instead of the
unfortunate one that they had by the fight of the sword, and more often by nothing, especially as they gave themselves quarter, will never
fail, or very seldom, in this fight to have both because for one, there
is no fear of them escaping, considering that if the pistol misses the
sword will not fail to finish the other.

But I don't doubt that someone is offended and says only that this
comparison is ridiculous and that there is a great difference between
desperate persons who kill themselves voluntarily and men of condition, who carry themselves in these very perilous combats, who
through them make them see the grandeur of their courage, especially
since the more frightful these combats are, the more this increases for
them renown and epithets of valiant, bold and noble.

But make such difference as one would like, according to me (with

---

[104] *à brusle pourpoint ou à brusle chemise*

regard to the effect) I do not find any at all.

Yet to reason well, why give these epithets to these combatants about who boast of them so much, since so many girls, women and men who have been killed deserve as much or more? And as witness to my words, I refer to the stories of the ancient philosophers and stoics who praise so highly the nobility and courage of so many girls and women and men for giving themselves voluntarily and with their own hands the mortal blows which they plunge into their hearts in diverse ways, by which they ended their days, because there is much more greatness of heart and of courage in taking one's life oneself than in allowing it to be taken by another. See with what admiration they speak of Cato, Scipio and an infinity of others of both sexes who have torn out their lives with their own hands by various kinds of death.

If, therefore, the Ancients earned these praises, why, humanly speaking, do those of today not merit them as well since they follow them and end their lives in the same ways?

But, one will say to me, there is a great difference because those then were Pagans and these now are Christian, who are forbidden on pain of eternal damnation from thus killing themselves.

This is why we can say (since one holds that the more the man puts himself on frightening precipices, the more he increases his label of courage)[105] that Pagans are still more noble than them [knife fighters], because those Pagans had only to overcome the difficulties of the torments of death which they gave themselves and these [Christian knife fighters] have the torments of death and hell.

Therefore, no one has reason to be offended if I say that the puny girls and sissies[106] who are being killed by their own hands and by their own wills deserve, despite their handguns on foot, as much and more to have all the titles of great hearts, since they fear neither the horrors of death, the infernal torments nor the eternal torments of hell into which they throw themselves as boldly as the most valiant of all these combatants.

In truth, the Devil lit upon one subtle invention, having put into the heads of men to end their quarrels with pistol shots and on foot, and that they cannot give quarter so they cannot escape from each other. He must have jumbled the brains of those who introduced a combat so ridiculous and so full of brutality.

Yes, I say ridiculous, just as if two men who would play to end their quarrel with strength or with a roll of the dice, provided that whoever wins would kill the loser. If that were the case, wouldn't everyone say

---

[105] *grand cœur*
[106] *femmelettes*

that these two characters would be ridiculous, crazy and brainless, and hate to see them play with their lives, their honour and their souls in a game whose winning depends only on strength or chance?

And yet this is what our combatants are doing today, playing a game that is as ridiculous and more detestable than the above, especially since in playing dice everyone would hope to win [against] his companion and ultimately there would be only one to lose his life.

But in this game of pistols, those who play it can only hope to come back even. But also, it is very certain that this game, being well played (as each puts into it the best pains he can do), creates havoc for both, which makes them both lose at the same time and, as the wager, there stands their bodies and souls.

Well, isn't here a beautiful but rather crazy game of chance and strength, worthy of great praise to those who play such pledges?

But notwithstanding all that can be said about it, this combat is well rooted in the heads of French,[107] and, previously, we have seen the greatest who have left their wagers, without speaking about the number of mediocre persons who have also lost theirs on one side or the other and even those who had made twenty or thirty combats with the sword from the first time they stood there.

That which gives great contentment to many unskilled [persons] who, not being able, by their feigning, laziness and negligence, to ascend and achieve the skill and valour of combat with the sword, knew (through the help of the Devil) to introduce and put into fashion this combat with the handgun and little knife, and to bring down all the valiant and noble with their skill, which they could not attain, and put and reduce them [ie: the skilled] with them [ie: the unskilled] to a measure equivalence and equality.[108]

Have they not found a subtle means of removing from the skilled, both with the sword and on horse, all the subtleties of their exercise which they have learned with such care, work and expense to preserve their life and honour? For, after all, those that play with them with a single stroke of chance, instead of a chance for one, wins both?

Without lying, I very much pity the simplicity of these poor skilled [persons], who strip themselves to imitate and run the same risk and the same inconvenience as those who are all naked by necessity, who are doing a ridiculous thing which shocks all reason. Like a man who has used his work for a number of years, through which he has earned goods and conveniences to live the rest of his days at his ease, strips

---

[107] *nos François*. I cannot find a suitable bundle of *François*-es to direct this at, so I decide to aim it at the French people.

[108] *en balance équilibre et ligne parallèle*. The metaphor is to a set of balance scales

himself of them and leaves them there unused to put himself among the ranks of the needy and lazy, who throughout their lives have not wanted to work, in order to make him suffer and endure such pains and inconveniences as them.

What I am saying here is not that I want to support or approve of sword duels, whether done on horseback, or those of the handgun done on foot. On the contrary, I detest them all, knowing full well that they are equally forbidden by all divine and human laws and that whoever loses his life in this, whether by pistol or by sword, on foot or on horse, one is well worth the other.[109] But, as they say of two evils, one must avoid the worst, and as there are more lazy [persons] than hard-working, similarly against a skilled [person], there will be a hundred unskilled who all can [pistol duel] where there is no quarter and where all the opponents make themselves perish in an instant.

Finally, I do not know by what blindness the skilful allow themselves to be suckered in and carried away in this ridiculous fight, and the more I think about it, the more it astonishes me, when I consider that people of great condition who have passed a number of years in academies learning the exercises of handling their swords and riding horses, and having rendered by their work most skilful, they fail in the end when it comes to settling a quarrel, because the sword of the skilful man is useless to him, and although well mounted on a good horse that he will know to ride as he can, it will also be necessary to please and satisfy the clumsy man with sword and horse, who dismounts and puts feet on the ground, takes his saddle pistols,[110] and ties up or leaves his horse there, and he leaves his equipment behind to make a pistol shot.

Isn't this a civil and orderly fight? Isn't it nice to see two horsemen of this kind circling on foot, one opposite the other, shooting each other and both thrown down?

Ah, if the skilful ones should take my advice, I would advise them (as it is necessary to do) of two things, namely, that if their opponents refused to fight against them with the sword alone, that they oblige them (as to the place they choose the fight with the pistol) to do it at least on horseback, to relieve their legs, and keep their shoes, and that if they refused both, taking as an excuse that they refused both, taking as an excuse that they would have no skill with the sword or on horseback, to make a great blow with baton against them, as [they are] unworthy of carrying any other weapon or the name of knight.

---

[109] *l'un vaut bien l'autre* (lit) the one is worth the other
[110] *ses pistolets de d'arçon*

How Combat With Pistols Damages the King and His Status

It is still not enough to say that pistol duels are only detrimental to those who do them. I want to show the damage that it does to the King, and to all his state, and how it takes away from him that which maintains and sustains him.

For no one can deny that the greatest and most powerful force and power of Kings and Republics is the great multitude of their subjects. This multitude of subjects has no strength or power to support Kings and Republics against those who dare to attack them if they are not educated and cannot use and handle with skill all kinds of weapons. So it is necessary for Kings and Republics to have and maintain, for their preservation, masters who show and teach their subjects to handle well and deftly use all kinds of weapons.

We see from this argument that the sovereign power of a King depends on the skill of his subjects, and the skill of the subjects on the teaching of fencing masters and others who show them to direct and spur on their horses.

And, as a consequence of which, all those who take away the teaching and skill of arms from the subjects are enemies who greatly offend the King, since they bash, destroy and put to nothing everything that maintains and sustains his reign and his state, and which consequently leave him to the free license and plunder of his adversaries by not being able to resist them.

This is what our combatants do today with handguns and small knives on foot, which are weapons that all kinds of people can use without learning and with which the truest ruffian can kill the greatest, the most valiant, and the most skillful man that can be found on earth.

By such combat they destroy and annihilate all the other exercises and skill of the French. Yet it is no longer necessary to speak of learning any exercise of arms, whether high or low, nor to ride a horse, and neither masters nor academies are necessary any longer to teach them, since the fashion has come and been introduced to finish quarrels with pistol shots on foot. It is so in fashion that it is not only persons of the most vile and base condition, but even children of nine or ten years, who have their pockets full of pistols and who want to blow their noses at the most valiant man in the universe at the slightest word which displeases them.

Will one not admit to me that it is a very pernicious, wicked and unhappy invention of duelling which brings and will bring into

France an infinity of misfortunes and disorders, which will strip the King (if God does not grant him the Grace to remedy it) of all his subject's skill, which is His greatest strength and power, which has made His entire state formidable to all other foreign nations? Principally so in battles, when they went to fight against [their enemies], both cavalry and infantry, and which, after the first discharge of their muskets, gave head down, sword in hand, littering the bodies of their opponents, pierced and beaten in such great quantity that, in short, nothing could escape them, nor resist this manner of fighting?

I believe that our pistoleers on foot[111] would not care to undertake to do or win such victories with their pistols as has been done by those with their swords alone, [whose blades] have passed through the stomachs of an infinite number of musketeers and cannoneers and remain masters of the battlefield and all their [ie: the pistoleers] artilleries.

And if someone said that fighting with pistols does not prevent the King's subjects from learning all the other exercises of arms, both on foot and on horse, I answer and show that it does, and that it destroys them entirely. For is it not true that before the introduction of this fighting, each according to his condition learned to handle and use, with skill, the weapons which were proper and suitable for the preservation and defence of his life and honour?

People of high condition went to the academies where they used their cares and work in order to make them more skilled to spur and train their horses, and to make sword strikes on foot and on horse in order to defend themselves when they would be attacked by persons of their condition, neighbours or others, and to serve their prince and country. Those who carry the sword learn for the same objective to use it in need and in encounters.

The inhabitants of the towns learn likewise the exercise of high arms, namely, the pike, halberd and *espadon*, or two-handed sword, which are good weapons, proper and suitable to them, in order to prevent the disorders which happen in their towns or defend their walls against the enemy and preserve their persons. And when a charge[112] is made with a halberd, twenty or thirty swords can be put away without any inconvenience.

The haberdashers, boilermakers and others of low condition learn from one another to play with their double-ended batons,[113] with which they do marvels at assemblies and fairs when sedition occurs.

The valets and grain winnowers living in the houses of nobility

---

[111] *nos pistoletiers à pied*
[112] *un sortait*
[113] *leurs bâtons à deux bouts*

similarly learn to handle staves, which the carry when hunting, with which a single well-trained person has beaten ten without instruction.

And generally speaking, all who have made themselves experts in skilfully using the weapons which are proper and suitable for them, with which they finish their quarrels and finally end them with nobility, he who is found the strongest forgave the weakest and was content when the victory was yielded and afterwards they became great friends.

But who today will invite knights to spend twenty-four years working during this time on their minds and bodies, using their money uselessly in the academies, since it can be of no service to them in their quarrels, the fashion being to end them with pistol shots and on foot and whoever refuses to do so and wants to use his skill passes for a cowardly man without heart?

Similarly, what good is it for the inhabitants to learn to play with high weapons since when they want to use them in order to put down some mutiny in the town, they only serve themselves to be shot in the head (by some rogue) with a pistol, and so on.

Therefore, who does not see that I have reason to say that the use of pistols destroys and slaughters all good exercise and strips the French of their former skill and valour and envelops them in ignorance which will metamorphose them from lions, which they were to foreign nations, into hinds and hares, which have no other subtlety for the preservation of their lives than to run well.

And in order to show that fighting with the handgun is not only dangerous in the singular, one man against another, but in general, several against several, I would ask that all these pistoleers, were they fifty thousand, what resistance could they make, being well arranged on a beautiful plain and battlefield, armed with pistols and little knives in the way that they fight.

Against four or five thousand men, half armed only with *espadons* of competent length and width and the other half with good halberds which they know how to use properly, who would also be well arranged in a large battalion and extended in front, maintaining a sufficiently spacious distance between their ranks and files in order to not inconvenience each other when using their weapons, and that all the leaders of the files were armed with *espadons* and covered with good thick cloaks which they put on going into the attack in several doubles and folds on the left arm, holding it forward, and the *espadon* in the right hand, walking forward together with a quick and light step, heads lowered, until being close to them and throwing off their cloaks, taking their *espadons* with both hands, doing all together and at one time, leap among them, making also round cuts, doubles and triples, with steps turning a half-turn to the right and a half-turn to the left and continuing thus until, being tired by their strikes and violent movements, another rank of halberdiers advances and takes their place while these retire between the files to the rear of these to catch their breath. And continuing thus, each rank supporting and refreshing the other until the end of the combat.

Ha! One would see them make, in an instant, beautiful openings among these bold pistoleers, legs and thighs cut, broken, bellies split and guts on the ground by their round cuts. How many broken elbows and sides and wrists cut and thrown away by their rising false edge simples and doubles,[114] heads split and quartered, shoulders battered and broken by their double and simple strikes, and, finally, the bodies one would see overthrown and pierced by their points and spears, notwithstanding all the prancing that these poor pistoleers could do.

It was this manner of fighting, which gives such astonishment, that Alexander the Great with the thirty or forty thousand well-trained and skilled Macedonians that he had in two or three pitched battles put more than four or five hundred thousand combatants (in each of these) of Darius, King of the Persians, and several others which afterwards he subjugated, on their bellies.

This is why the old Politicians, having clearly seen and noted that their strength and victories in these battles consisted not in the number of combatants but in their skill, sought and used their industry on all sides in order to have their subjects instructed in all types of exercises of arms and gave prizes to those who earned them through their skill with titles of praise, honour and glory which they carried above others in order to inspire and convince everyone to achieve them. This is still observed today in all the states of the sovereigns, but much more precisely in Turkey, who instruct the nurseries of the Janissaries, composed of children whom they raise by right of tribute, of three boys, one of which they put, when they have achieved in age and strength of handling all types of weapons, who are the guard and forces of the Great Sultan and of his Empire and who do wonders in battles.

Our former Dukes of Brittany also had an excellent way of doing things in their militia, which was that in each parish there was a number of men most capable of carrying arms, whom they called Free Archers, chosen by the votes of the principals of it, to whom he paid wages every year, both in times of peace and war. And when the

---

[114] *faux montants* – Italian fencing terms transliterated into French

Dukes needed it, they made and composed in two lots of twenty-four hours a strong and powerful army of people all well-made, skilful and noble. And in this way of doing things, they maintained themselves and made themselves indomitable to their neighbours and without doing wrong or inconvenience to the least of their subjects.

If this order were observed today in France, it would not be seen (it seems to me) so pillaged or ruined as it is by the soldiers,[115] that one takes with praise from foreign countries for the service of the King, and his Majesty would be served with much more affection, fidelity, strength and power than he is by these strangers, who seek and have no other affection than their [own] interests at the expense of his good subjects.

---

[115] *les gens de guerre*

Chapter IV

Where It Is Seen that the Devil is the Author of Combat with Pistols

I have previously shown by good and strong reasoning, the damage, misfortune and disorder that this new combat with handguns brings to France, both to the private individual and in general, for which I have attributed the fundamental cause to ignorance and awkwardness in the exercise of the sword, which is a common and honourable weapon to all those who carry it, being also indeed the most noble and ancient of all the others and the most cherished and esteemed by the great who always carry it by their side, as much as a mark of their greatness and quality as to preserve their persons against those who would like to offend them and of which, at all times, men have been very curious and careful to learn the exercise and skill because, at all times also, [it] has been the usual custom to end differences with it, and notwithstanding any prohibitions that the Church and the Kings may have made, and all the remedies that they have known to do and to bring to prevent these hateful fights and duels, which were all of no use. That makes one see and know that it is a fury from hell that the demon has put from the beginning[116] into the heads of men and now it is impossible to take it out of their imagination, preferring rather their honour than their bodies and their souls. But seeing that this sword fight was not yet sufficiently pernicious and profitable for the increase of his empire, he knew and wanted lately[117] to bring it [swordsmanship] down and abolish it because most often he was only wasting his time and his effort, considering that after having employed all his diabolical industries and subtlety to put dissension and quarrels between men and to make them go out onto the meadow to cut their throats, he saw that by thinking of deceiving them he was deceiving himself, especially since instead of carrying out his designs and intentions they ended an instant their old quarrels and enmity by disarming each other with skill and giving each other quarter and from the irreconcilable enemies that they were, they became great friends and, therefore, he was frustrated by their claims.

And in order to not fall into the same trap, what did he do? He removed from most men who make professions of honour the knowledge of and skill with their swords in order to afterwards use their ignorance as an opportunity to found, establish and put into fashion and to make them fight with handguns on foot in order that in this

---

[116] *de toute ancienneté*
[117] *depuis peu de jours*

his efforts would not be fruitless and so that instead of one he can have two. And in order to invite them to it, he made them believe and put into their imaginations that as much as these fights are horrible and dreadful, so much more do they raise up those who do them and put them above the common and give them epithets of great hearted, noble and bold and, on the contrary, blame and despise all those who want to use their swords and their skill, saying that they are cowards and heartless persons.

See how the devil is known to use ignorance to come to the object of his designs and to bring down the men of renown[118] in great evil.[119]

Let no one here ask me who moves me to make this speech or why since I have shows well enough how the demon uses all his power to abolish our exercise in order to and by this means increase his gain and profit, causing us to lose ours.

This is why with good reason, I oppose now the execution of his designs and will and make myself an inciter against him to make everyone see the pernicious tricks and treachery which he used to remove the cause which prevented its effects in order to disillusion all those whom he has deceived by a false mask and semblance of truth, which is no ordinary act, to deceive and cheat men more easily.

I have just said above that the demon, in order to establish and found this ridiculous and unfortunate fighting with pistols on foot and others even more detestable, has used ignorance without which he would never have achieved it.

And to keep people today in ignorance about our exercise, what did he do? He addressed fathers and mothers and others who have stewardship over youth, who are always naturally inclined and passionate about raising and preserving their children, making them see and consider several hazards and misfortunes which could happen to those who, being very skilled, sometimes meet in these sword fights, causing and giving great fear and apprehension to their parents. Then, he made them understand and believe, under the false appearance of truth, that it was only the skill which caused them all these disorders and that the chief means of preserving their children was to prevent them from doing and learning this exercise and skill with swords in order to remove boldness from them and render them cowards in order to have them live for a long time. And by this means conceived so subtly to slide this opinion into their imaginations that there is not one in a hundred today (to my belief) who do not maintain that this is

---

[118] *sieur* The translation is a guess to match the context

[119] *tomber ... en chaud mal.* Basically equivalent to "out of the frying pan and into the fire".

true. And thus how and through which means he opened the source
and origin of all the terrible fights where there can never be quarter
and if one escapes, it is only through extreme fortune or a miracle.

But this is not yet all. This demon is not content to put into the
fancy of men having themselves killed in fights with swords and pistols, he reinvents them every day, more ridiculous, pernicious and
damnable than those, and especially this one where they lock themselves in a room or between four walls, two against two, or even more,
and there slit each other's throats with many bayonets or kitchen
knives, so that none has any advantage or way to escape this peril,
nor the power to preserve his life.

Oh, well! Are these not the horrible manias and furies of hell,
which the demon has sowed among men to destroy for ever their
bodies and their souls, by ways so cruel, extraordinary and unheard
of? Has he not found some subtle endeavours to destroy all together
these poor miserable combatants?

And all this happened through the opinion (put by this wicked
demon) in the imagination of all the ancients, to whom having made
them believe that the sovereign means to preserve the youth and to
prevent him from going close to drawing the sword, was to take away
the skill and science of it.

This opinion was only too unfortunately followed and used, because this youth being cruel and grown in age although brought up
without skill, it did not prevent him from having enough heart and
courage to want to execute his passions, to avenge himself on the outrages which one did to him and be provoked on a point of honour. But
knowing himself weak and unfit for avenging these outrages through
combat with the sword, the demon, knowing how to alleviate this
fault, gave him, invented and put into his head doing all these horrible
fights, of which we have just spoken, where there is no skill other than
rage and despair, in order to envelop them together and throw them
in the infernal abyss in order to make them know eternally and detest
the grandeur of their heart, courage and valour and that as much as
that believe themselves elevated above the common man, they enclose
themselves below.

And to completely uproot this opinion from the heads of the vulgar, who believe that it is this skill which has caused these fights and
duels between men, I uphold and show the contrary and maintain that
it is hatred, treason and the desire for vengeance that the demon sowed
between them from the beginning of the world in order to destroy
each other through duels and fights (witness the story of Abel, who
was treacherously killed by his brother Cain with the jawbone of an

ass) who founded and invited men to carefully learn the exercise and skill of arms in order to repulse their enemies and preserve their lives.

And finally, it is not true to say that skill invites those who have it to seek out occasions to put it into practice and use because it is seen that all those who are the most expert and skilled are of the same humour as the most skillful and learned men who every day instruct and judge the trials of others, that we nevertheless see those who have the least in their private name, who hate them the more and who desire at least to have it and, having occasion and cause, who finish them more easily because they know and understand the pain, worry and expense with the uncertainty and all the difficulties that there is in ending them.

Also, one no longer usually sees that those who understand the least in business and in arms are the most opinionated and enterprising with the least cause, in lawsuits, quarrels and nitpicking,[120] where they put themselves so forward that in the end they cannot get out of it and who, thinking of ruining and losing their opponents,[121] ruin and lose themselves.

In closing,[122] I say that it is still and more necessary for a man to know the science and skill of handling his sword well for the preservation of his person, that knowing the science and practice of being well instructed and pursuing his trials in order to preserve his goods and his family, especially since all men that one knows to be expert in these two things prevented the most learned and bold from shocking him and attacking him inappropriately.

In such a manner, it is therefore quite the opposite to say that the exercise and skill at arms is prejudicial, since it is also as necessary and useful to anyone as is any other science, both for general preservation of the state as for each in particular.

I say again further that the exercise of arms, both high and low, is the best and most suitable to please and exercise youth than any other that one can seek or invent. For there is none that is so recreational, useful, necessary, which increases the strength and disposition of the body, which awakens the mind and the judgement, which is so clean of all vices, and which teaches the best [way] to live and conduct themselves civilly and wisely in company than this one, and where it takes the least time and money.

Because isn't it true that there would be much more pleasure and contentment for everyone seeing the youth of a city all together at feasts and Sundays (after having returned their duties to God) lined

---

[120]*chicaneries*
[121]*qui pensant ruiner et perdre leurs parties*
[122]*en partant*

up in beautiful battalions in some fine place of arms, where for recreation seeing them exercise, sometimes with the musket or arquebus, sometimes with the pike, formerly with the halberd and *espadon*, and at other times making assaults with foil against each other against whom some prize would be won. That to not see all these young people in the games of bowls, rolling wood, or elsewhere playing other games, the snacks[123] and their money, and beyond going to the cabarets to exercise the pots and the glasses, which to them is a greatly prejudicial and contrary exercise, considering that the youth is only too hot, boiling and prompt of itself, which makes taking wine a little in excess, ignites them in such a way the natural heat that it gives them back, raging and furious, and destroys them, brutalizes and takes away entirely spirit, judgement and all reason, with strength and vigour and disposition of the body. And finally it makes them capable of doing all kinds of vices and misfortunes, which strip them of all their goods and honour, throws them into necessity and misery, them and their parents.

And this is how most of today's youth are lost, for lack of honest exercise and occupation, entertaining themselves with all these debaucheries and misfortunes. And I am very surprised (if I am allowed to say so) like all those who have stewardship over the people and who govern the provinces, cities and communities, do not remedy all these disorders, and that they do not strive to have youth do all these beautiful and noble exercises with all kinds of weapons, which is an easy thing to do and at little cost and which would be greatly useful, necessary and beneficial to the King and his whole state, and which would give recreation, pleasure and contentment to all his subjects.

Finally, in conclusion, if all these reasons are not yet sufficient to remove from the heads of all those who say and maintain that it is the skill which leads and invites men to make all these unfortunate singular combats and duels, with which they destroy each other, and that these combats being a very pernicious effect on them, the cause which leads them there (which they say to be the skill) is also wicked and pernicious, which thus must be, according to their opinion, hated, abhorred, rejected and defended.

To which I will tell them again for the final reason that if this effect is bad, that it does not follow for this reason that the cause, which is in their imagination the skill, is not very good, useful and necessary, as I have here above shown it.

And that if their reason were as true as it is false, it would follow by

---

[123]*collations*

the same consequence that all the other sciences and studies which are in the world, would be similarly wicked, pernicious and greatly prejudicial, understanding that one has seen and are still seeing damnable effects. Witness an infinite number of Heretics, who by their studies, sciences and doctrines, have lost and infected by them the greatest part of men and consequently they should also be defended and prevented from studying and learning all the other sciences, all the more so as they have been and are the cause of the perdition and damnation of most of them.

LongEdge Press

LongEdge Press publishes quality translations of French texts of interest to the scholar and practitioner of historical fencing. Visit LongEdge Press at www.longedgepress.com for more books, articles on items of historical interest and practical guides.

Secrets of the Sword Alone Henri de Sainct-Didier (1573)

Fencing Through the Ages Adolphe Corthey (1898), including his report on the *Transformation de l'Épée de Combat* (1894) and several contemporary newspaper reports of his public demonstrations of historical fencing.

La Canne Royale Larribeau, Humé, comprising Larribeau's *Nouvelle Théorie du Jeu de la Canne* (1856) and Humé's *Traité et Théorie de Canne Royale* (1862)

The Art of Fencing Jean de Brye (1721)

Fencing Manual Ministry of War (1877)

Manual of Contre-Pointe Fencing Joseph Tinguely (1856) with a foreword by Julian Garry of *De Taille et d'Estoc*

Archives of the Masters of Arms of Paris Henry Daressy (1888)

www.ingramcontent.com/pod-product-compliance
Lightning Source LLC
Chambersburg PA
CBHW031002090426
42737CB00008B/647